PATTERNS OF MANAGEMENT
IN LOCAL GOVERNMENT

Government and Administration Series
Edited by F.F RIDLEY, Professor of Political Theory and Institution
University of Liverpool

Implementation in a Bureaucracy
The Execution Process *Volume 1*
ANDREW DUNSIRE

Control in a Bureaucracy
The Execution Process *Volume 2*
ANDREW DUNSIRE

Public Administration and the Law
GAVIN DREWRY

The Government of Education
KEITH FENWICK and PETER MCBRIDE

Policy Analysis
W. I. JENKINS

Governing under Pressure
J. J. RICHARDSON and A. G. JORDAN

Government and Administration in Europe
edited by F. F. RIDLEY

Administration and the State
BRIAN C. SMITH and G. D. WOOD

The Politics of the Firm
LEONARD TIVEY

PATTERNS OF MANAGEMENT IN LOCAL GOVERNMENT

Royston Greenwood, Kieron Walsh
C. R. Hinings and Stewart Ranson

MARTIN ROBERTSON • OXFORD

First published in 1980 by Martin Robertson, Oxford.

ISBN 0 85520 244 0 (case edition)
ISBN 0 85520 245 9 (paperback edition)

Typeset by Pioneer Associates Ltd., East Sussex
Printed and bound by Richard Clay (The Chaucer Press) Ltd.,
Bungay, Suffolk

Contents

CHAPTER 1   The Study of Local Authorities   1

CHAPTER 2   From the Committee on Management (1967) to the Bains Working Group (1973)   12

CHAPTER 3   Local Authorities in the Post-Reorganization Period   32

CHAPTER 4   Eight Patterns of Management   67

CHAPTER 5   Why Do Local Authorities Differ? Why Do They Change?   92

CHAPTER 6   The Impacts of Situational Contingencies   125

CHAPTER 7   Conclusions   156

References   173

Index   181

CHAPTER 1

The Study of Local Authorities

INTRODUCTION

Any attempt to understand the British political system cannot afford to ignore local government. Local authorities play a large and an increasingly important part in governing the country. They spend a large proportion — almost eighteen per cent — of the Gross National Product and employ about twelve per cent of the nation's workforce. These resources are used to provide a variety of essential services ranging from education, social welfare and housing, to the more mundane necessities of refuse collection and disposal. The claim for the importance of local government does not, however, rest solely on the pragmatic basis of the scale and significance of the services it provides. Moral and philosophical arguments have been made for the value of local government in promoting democracy and individual liberty. Sharpe (1970) in a discussion of the contemporary role of local government, concludes that:

> . . . the participatory value if not the liberty value still remains as a valid one for modern local government. Not perhaps in the full glory of its earlier promoters but as an important element in modern democracy nonetheless. [p. 174]

Local government, in short, has a significance both as provider and administrator of basic services, and as a promoter of certain values. It is important, therefore, to understand how the local government system operates. The study of local government has been approached from a variety of viewpoints, employing different concepts and using a range of methods and intents. It is not the purpose here to review the range of available approaches, but it is necessary to make clear both the focus of the present text (what it

1

is that we seek to understand) and the approach (the concepts and methods that will be used to facilitate understanding).

The focus of the present book is the organizational structure of the local authority. That structure represents part of the decision framework of the authority. We wish to know what that structure (or decision framework) looks like, and, perhaps more importantly, *why* that framework looks as it does.

The organizational decision structure of a local authority encompasses two elements. Local authorities operate through committees and departments, and with various kinds of permanent or temporary groups. The configuration of these committees, departments and groups is popularly depicted in the organization chart. This formal configuration is the first element of structure with which we are concerned. Committees and departments, however, are linked through procedures and conventions which spell out the ways in which different parts of the authority interact. Thus, the relationship between the chief executive and fellow chief officers, or between the management team and the policy committee, are detailed either in formal procedures, or working conventions. The second aspect of the local authority decision structure, in other words, is the pattern of organizational interactions. For our purposes, then, we would define the organizational structure of the local authority as the *configuration* of committees, departments, and groups, plus the pattern of *interactions* linking these organizational parts.

The study of local authority structures, especially of the configuration of committees, departments, and groups, is not new. There exists a series of papers discussing the events and actions within particular authorities (Smith, 1965; Basildon, 1966; Elliott, 1971; Haynes, 1978; Haywood, 1977; Kinch, 1974) in addition to a range of texts detailing the internal organization of authorities generally (Richards, 1968, 1978; Jackson, 1965; Cross, 1970; Knowles, 1977; Redcliffe-Maud and Wood, 1974). This latter literature — texts covering authorities generally — usually adopt what may be termed the legal—institutional approach. It is worth commenting upon two of the weaknesses commonly found in this approach because the present book was largely prompted by dissatisfaction with it. The focus of the present book will become clearer from an understanding of the disadvantages of the legal—institutional perspective.

The legal—institutional approach focuses upon the local government system as a whole. It aims to describe and discuss the legal and institutional framework within which local government must operate. This framework is clearly important. It represents the operational ground rules for local authority undertakings. Local authority structures are inevitably dependent upon the rules and regulations embodied in various Acts of Parliament. By describing and elucidating the provisions of these acts, the broad context within which local government authorities operate can be set. The legal—institutional approach, in other words, is a valuable preliminary for understanding the way that local authorities are structured. They give the basic legal facts and describe the ground rules. But they do little beyond this. Two things are lacking: first, a consideration of the *complexity and variation* of local authority structures; secondly, an ability to account for *changes* that occur over time.

The structures of local authorities vary considerably. Despite their common legal framework authorities operate with different numbers and types of departments and committees, they establish different ways of ensuring co-ordination, they link officers and members in different ways, and so on. Admittedly, there are similarities, some imposed by statute. But the constraints on organizational arrangements set by statute are drawn widely (Garner, 1973) and as a result there is much variation between authorities. In some instances the variation may concern a specific part of the organization: for example, authorities vary according to whether they have a chief executive or not, whether they have an independent finance committee, whether the recreation function is combined within the education committee, and so on. In other cases there are important variations in the broad style of the authority: for example, in the next chapter a contrast is drawn between concentrated and deconcentrated systems of organization. These important differences are not covered by the institutional approach.

Those who adopt the institutional approach do not deny the

existence or importance of inter-authority variation. Thus, Richards (1973) acknowledges that

> The conventions that develop within the formal structure of a local authority have a great effect upon the way in which business is carried through and how decisions are made. [p. 123]

Nevertheless, what these variations are, and how they affect the transaction of business, are questions that are rarely considered. And yet the importance of the variations may be illustrated quite easily. Consider, for example, the development of area-based approaches (Hambleton, 1977, 1978; Mason, 1978) to management and policy making. A number of authorities have begun to experiment with structures intended to overcome the fragmentation often associated with a division of labour based upon service committees and departments. Thus, a number have set up area committees, or sub-committees (see pp. 42—5). Authorities with these types of sub-committees obviously intended that the pattern of decision-making should be much more decentralized than would occur under more traditional arrangements. They also intended that the operations of the authority should be responsive to community preferences and involvement. How far these approaches are successful is a matter of empirical inquiry but it can be safely concluded that structural differences of this kind are likely to be important for the pattern of decision-making and influence within the authority. The first major failing, then, of the institutional approach is that it neglects variations between the decision structures of local authorities, variations that may well have important consequences for the involvement of councillors and members, for the pattern of decision-making, and, ultimately, the balance of service provision.

The second failing is that the approach is largely static: it ignores, or gives cursory treatment to, the way that authorities change and develop, even within an unchanging institutional environment. And yet, it is evident that local authorities are persistently reviewing and altering their structures. These changes may be specific and affect limited parts of the organization: for example, recent years have seen the dismissal of a small number of chief executives (Lomer, 1977). On the other hand, there are widely publicized instances of authorities that have undergone extensive and thoroughgoing internal reorganizations (for example,

Liverpool in 1969 following the appointment of management consultants — see Greenwood and Stewart, 1974). These structural changes are both important and interesting yet are largely absent within the legal-institutional approach.

The present book attempts to avoid these weaknesses. The focus, as already noted, is the organizational structure of the local authority. But the emphasis will be upon differences and similarities of structure, and upon how those similarities and differences alter over time. The complexity and instability of local authority organizational arrangements is mapped in Chapters 3 and 4, and then there follows an attempt to explain that complexity and instability. The book seeks not merely to describe local authority structures, showing how and to what extent structures may vary, but also to offer some explanation of why structures vary from authority to authority, and why changes take place. *In particular, it explores how far structural variation and change exist in English local government, and the extent to which that variation and change may be explained by the situational circumstances (or 'contingencies' as they are labelled below) of the local authority.*

Before describing how the above purpose will be tackled an important question should be answered. The question is whether the study of local authority structures *by itself* is a useful endeavour. Is the span of attention unduly restricted if discussion focuses exclusively upon matters of structure? Should other variables figure in the analysis? In a way these questions strike at a central assumption of the following chapters, which is, that the organizational structures of local authorities are important determinants both of the ways in which decisions are made and of the content of those decisions. Structures, it is assumed here, help shape decisions reached and actions taken. Such an assumption, of course, is consistent with the recent behaviours of local authorities. Authorities have persistently changed their committee and departmental arrangements to remove unwanted disadvantages and secure desired opportunities. Thus, a considerable proportion of authorities have changed their structures in pursuit of a 'corporate approach'. Some of these structural reorganizations are documented in Chapter 2, and analysed at a later juncture. The assumption is also consistent with the observations and recommendations of a series of government reports, from the Report of the Committee on Management in 1967, to the reports of the Bains

Working Group (1972) and the Paterson Advisory Group (1973). In these reports there is an evident belief that alternative structures produce, or contribute to, alternative results. Structures, in other words, are believed to matter.

It is not sufficient, of course, to justify an assumption on the grounds that it is held by others: that way orthodoxy prevails and development is stifled. Moreover, there have been clear warnings against an obsession with structure. Stewart, for example, in his usual pithy way, advises that 'to change structures without changing the process it is designed to sustain is an empty action' (1971, p. 25). Stewart is right to warn of an undue concern with structure. But to recognize, as he does, that other factors are important is not to say that structure is unimportant. On the contrary, the principal thrust of Stewart's criticism is not that structure is *un*important but that it is one of several important variables. In other words, structure is important and requires examination. But does it demand examination separately from the study of other variables? The answer rests with the concern of the investigator. On the one hand, the student may probe the relationship between structure and various ideas about performance. He may examine the relationship between various patterns of organization and, for example, the promotion of co-ordinated and efficient decision taking. Does the concept of an executive office, as put forward by the Paterson Advisory Group hinder or assist a co-ordinated approach to policy making? Does the existence of a management team of chief officers coupled with a strong chief executive reduce the measure of democracy by limiting the involvement and influence of elected representatives? These and similar questions represent one line of inquiry.

A second line of inquiry would proceed with rather different questions. What are the constraints which limit the potential utility of alternative structures? What difference does it make to be a large rather than small local authority? Can a large local authority employ the same kind of committee and departmental organization as that of a much smaller local authority, even if both authorities seek similar goals of co-ordination and efficiency? What are the structural consequences of a council that is electorally unstable, with the complexion of the majority political party liable to shift between elections? There is a strong case for expecting local authorities to be constrained by their situational context. Before an authority can debate the relevance of any structural model the authority must recognize the 'requirements' imposed by the situation facing the authority. This may be easily illustrated. Many local authorities have, in recent years, sought to introduce a system of corporate planning. It is unrealistic, however, to expect all authorities to develop the *same* system. Rather, they have to develop a system appropriate to the size of the authority, the politics of the authority, and so on. Questions that follow from this line of inquiry would be of the following type: what kind of structures are appropriate for larger rather than smaller structures? what are the structural constraints imposed by various forms of political organization?

To follow the first line of inquiry would probably (but not inevitably) require consideration of variables other than structure. There would be merit in disentangling the relative effects of structural and processual variables. The latter line of inquiry, however, clearly does not necessitate the inclusion of processual variables. It is because our concern is with the relationship between structures and their context, rather than with structures and their effects, that we feel justified in studying organizational structures as a discrete exercise.

CONCEPTS AND METHODS

The concepts that will be used are largely drawn from the literature of organizational theory rather than that of political science. In particular, they are from what is becoming increasingly referred to as 'contingency theory' (Kast and Rosenzweig, 1973; Lupton, 1971). Contingency theory is concerned with the relationship between structures and situational context. The underlying hypothesis is that an organization must develop a set of structures appropriate to its context if it is to secure optimum performance. The organization has to achieve a 'goodness of fit' between its structure and context. In particular, it is often argued that three contingencies (that is, parts of the context) are of especial importance: the organizational *environment*, the *size* of the organization, and the *technology* employed.

The intellectual history of these arguments is not important here: interested readers should consult Child (1972) or Lupton (1971). Of rather greater concern is the assumption underlying them: that the performance of an organization is in part dependent upon the relevance of the organization's structures for the situational contingencies faced by that organization. As Kast and Rosenzweig (1973) put it, contingency views are 'ultimately directed towards suggesting organizational designs and managerial actions most appropriate for specific situations' (p. 313).

There are various difficulties and ambiguities within contingency theory as it has been practised. Not least is the tendency to ignore the question of why some organizations do not adapt their structures to situational constraints. For example, Woodward's researchers (1965) found that as many firms had *inappropriate* structures (that is, had not secured a 'goodness of fit') as had appropriate arrangements. There has been little effort to explain these organizational 'failures'. Child (1971) has suggested that the answer to this conundrum lies within the organization, in terms of the political forces that operate in all organizations: 'this simple theory is inadequate, primarily because it fails to give due attention to the agency of choice by whoever have the power to direct the organization' (p. 2). Powerful actors within an organization can choose an organizational strategy, even if their choice is inappropriate. We tend to agree with this interpretation, although we have reservations about the relative emphasis and meaning attributed to the idea of 'strategic choice'. Nevertheless, there are *two* sources of explanation for the development of organizational structures: 'external' contingencies, and the 'internal' processes of choice and deliberation by powerful personnel. In this book our predominant concern is with the former source of explanation, that is, with external contingencies. It is not our purpose to explore the relative importance of internal organizational processes.

It is a basic contention of later chapters, then, and the organizing principle of the material presented that the structures of a local authority may be examined and explained, at least in part, in terms of various situational contingencies. In making that contention we are attempting the study of political organizations using an approach that has been developed extensively in the study of industrial organizations. This application of ideas and concepts from the literature of organizational theory to that of public administration is not a process that receives universal approval. A number of writers have considered the applicability of such concepts and have reached differing conclusions. Some such as Dunsire (1973) are clearly in agreement; others such as Brown (1970) and Baker (1972) are sympathetic but cautious. Some, notably Self (1972), are openly critical and refer to the relatively 'inchoate' political processes of public agencies which render the concepts and logic of organizational analysis of limited value.

It is not unreasonable to expect that government bureaucracies will be different from their non-public counterparts. They are required to meet pressures of a political form to a much greater extent than they are required to meet pressures of a more strictly economic form. Manufacturing organizations, to a greater degree than is evident in either central or local government, operate with relatively straightforward economic criteria. Local authorities, on the other hand, are multi-functional organizations with a variable set of aims and goals. These can be reconciled only through the value choices of the political process, and measurement of organizational performance and success is an 'essentially contested' procedure. For this reason it would be unwise to adopt the particular concepts, or (perhaps more importantly) *only* those concepts that figure in the works of writers concerned with, and informed by, manufacturing or business organizations. The existing concepts of contingency theory, in other words, cannot be applied uncritically to the study of local authorities. A measure of reconsideration and a reworking of those concepts is inevitable. Nevertheless, our view is that the framework of contingency theory if not its details is sufficiently fertile to support its application to the study of local government. What is needed is a measure of reconceptualization rather than rejection.

The focus of this book has already been described as the relationship between structures and situational constraints. The conceptual framework, therefore, must include some way of discussing structures, and some way of discussing the constraints. The framework is developed in Chapters 2 and 5. Chapter 2 focuses upon the concepts of differentiation and integration, showing how these may be used to analyse organizational structures. The principal aim of that chapter is to clarify what these concepts mean and how they will be handled in later chapters. A subsidiary aim of Chapter 2 will be to trace the relevance and salience of differentiation and integration within the recent history of English local government. By summarizing the major reports and debates of the past few years it is hoped to demonstrate that the concepts, although sounding unfamiliar and perhaps strange, are actually to do with widely discussed and relevant issues. Chapter 5 explains more fully the approach of contingency theory and the various modifications and reformulations employed in this book. The chapter does not set out to provide the reader with a comprehensive summary of the contingency literature: instead, it focuses on the use made of that theory in Chapters 6 and 7. That is, Chapter 5 puts forward the contingencies that might be expected to set limits on the relevance of organizational structures.

Chapters 3, 4, 6 and 7 contain the results of our researches. Chapter 3 describes the organizational practices of local authorities in England and Wales. Using the ideas of differentiation and integration the amount of variation and similarity that exists throughout local government and the principal changes that have developed in recent years are described. The material presented in these chapters is taken from a survey of all local authorities conducted in 1977-8. Information was received from 412 of 455 authorities.

The results of a questionnaire survey have been interpreted with the advantage of additional material from a more detailed, four-year study of twenty-seven local authorities. The results of this study are set out elsewhere (Greenwood *et al.*, 1977; Hinings *et al.*, 1980) and it is not intended to draw extensively upon all aspects of that study. Here it is important to note that twenty-seven authorities were studied in 1974-8 to identify the ways in which organizational and policy-making arrangements actually operate and how and why they change. Inevitably, the interpretation of the questionnaire results has been partly shaped and assisted by this more detailed investigation of a limited number of authorities. Indeed, the initial design of the questionnaire was framed by the ideas and experiences coming from the twenty-seven case studies. Wherever possible relevant material from the study of twenty-seven local authorities is used to illustrate and interpret the questionnaire material. *

*This does *not* mean that authorities cited in the text are necessarily part of the sample of twenty-seven. We have quite deliberately included several references to authorities not in the sample, and where alternative illustrations are available, have avoided references to authorities that are in the sample.

The questionnaire survey permits us to show how far local authority structures vary, and to pinpoint areas of widespread similarity. By itself, however, the questionnaire cannot reveal changes that have occurred over the past decade, or which may occur in the next few years. To show patterns of change we have to compare the 1977-8 material with the practices of earlier years. Fortunately, there are a number of earlier studies that can be used for this purpose. The Committee on Management (1967) commissioned and published an extensive survey of local authority practices as they existed in 1964-5. Studies by Greenwood *et al.* (1969) summarize changes to local authority structures in the years immediately following publication of the Committee's Report. It is these surveys that provide our knowledge of local authority structures before the 1974 reorganization of local government.

Knowledge of developments since 1974 is available from two sources. The study of twenty-seven authorities provides insights into the problems and difficulties being experienced, and knowledge of any structural changes made, proposed, or imminent within those authorities. From this information we can make rather more than tentative judgments about current lines of thought and possible trends. Secondly, material is available from a survey of all local authorities carried out in 1974.* The sum total is material that provides sufficient evidence from which to tease out the fundamental shifts in structural practices that have occurred since 1974, and/or might occur in future years.

Chapters 6 and 7 seek to *explain* both the structural variations noted in Chapters 3 and 4, and the changes of the past fourteen years. How far the approach in this book succeeds in its attempt to explain local authority structures will be assessed in the concluding chapter. That chapter provides a review of the relative salience of external contingencies and the potential importance of internal political processes.

---

*Some of the results of the 1974 survey appeared in Greenwood *et al.* (1975) and Hinings *et al.* (1975).

CHAPTER 2

From the Committee on Management (1967) to the Bains Working Group (1974)

INTRODUCTION

Local authorities have considerable discretion over how they shall organize themselves in order to meet their responsibilities. There are, it is true, constraints imposed by statute. Councillors are required to operate collectively, whether through the full council or its sub-groups, such as committees and sub-committees, rather than individually (ministerially) as in central government. Particular committees must be set up and certain officers appointed. Nevertheless these constraints are widely drawn. As the Committee on Management pointed out, 'the internal organisation of a local authority is not codified in the law; it is a blend of statutory provisions and of custom and practice' (1967, p. 23). This is still the case. In matters of organization, at least, there is local rather than central control.

The consequence of local discretion is local variation. Local authorities differ in the number and pattern of committees and sub-committees they set up, the number of members who sit on each committee, the extent to which committees are linked through central policy committees, and the extent to which the policy committee is controlled by the majority political party. They differ also in the number of departments through which services are managed, the extent and range of central co-ordinating functions, and the role of the chief executive officer. There are differences in the way officers and members interact. Some authorities have established officer-member groups; some channel all items of policy through the management team of chief officers before they are discussed at member level; some have officers in attendance at political party meetings. Some authorities do none of these things.

Not all differences are important. What is needed at the outset, therefore, is a framework of ideas and concepts that will enable the observer to make sense of the details and complexities of organizational variation. The framework that we propose to use is set out below. The following chapter applies this framework to local authorities in England and Wales.

FOUR DIMENSIONS OF ORGANIZATIONAL STRUCTURE

There are two organizational or managerial processes which face all local authorities. First, there is the need to create committees and departments to cope with the sheer range and volume of work. Authorities provide too many services, and on too large a scale for all decisions to be taken at full council: there is an inevitable need for delegation of powers to committees, and sub-committees. Similarly, there is a need for several departments. This process, is referred to hereinafter as *structural differentiation.* It is, quite simply, the splitting of the local authority into bits. Once created, however, committees and departments have a tendency to pull in contrary directions. The inevitable result of differentiation is a centrifugal impetus which leads to at least some degree of operational fragmentation. The second process common to all authorities, therefore, is the creation of structural machinery that will counteract the pressures towards fragmentation. This process, of appointing co-ordinating committees, or management teams of chief officers, or central departments, is the process of *structural integration.*

Differentiation and integration are useful starting points for the analysis of structural characteristics. They refer to issues and dilemmas common to all organizations, and they have become increasingly important in the recent history of local authorities. It may be useful to summarize the salient features of this recent history, as from it a number of conceptual distinctions may be made. These distinctions are important for subsequent analysis and discussion. That history will also demonstrate that these structural concepts are not irrelevant to the practical world of local government, but, on the contrary, reflect the concerns and ideas of both members and officers.

For convenience the Report of the (Maud) Committee on Management of Local Government (1967) will be taken as the point of departure. That Report is a watershed in the development of local authority structures as it marked the end of a period of growing dissatisfaction with traditional administrative arrangements, but during which comparatively little administrative reform occurred, and the beginning of a period of accelerating administrative change. The nature of that later movement for change, moreover, was substantially shaped by the Committee's analysis. It is suggested below that the Committee's recommendations marked a distinct shift in emphasis towards the need for policy, as opposed to administrative, co-ordination, a shift maintained in subsequent developments. For these reasons the choice of 1967, the year in which the Committee's Report appeared, as the starting point, is both convenient and appropriate.

The Committee on Management of Local Government was set up in 1964

> to consider in the light of modern conditions how local government might best continue to attract and retain people (both elected representatives and principal officers) of the calibre necessary to ensure its maximum effectiveness. [p. iii]

These terms of reference were widely drawn, and widely interpreted. The Committee's Report included discussion of such topics as central—local relations, and relations between local authorities and the public. Perhaps its major influence, however, was upon the 'internal organization' of local authorities. The Committee's diagnosis was simple, and to the point:

> There is a long tradition of associating a particular committee with a specific service and this is hardened by the requirement of statutes that for certain services specific committees should be set up. The power which local authorities have (under section 85 of the 1933 Act) to delegate their functions to committees is a convenience for a council and indeed is often regarded as necessary for the transaction of business. But delegation disperses direction and control amongst a number of separate committees. There exists therefore in local authorities in this country an organisation which is based on separate parts in each of which there is gathered the individual service, with its professional departmental hierarchy led by a principal officer

and, supervising it, a committee of members. There may be unity in the parts, but there is disunity in the whole. [p. 26]

Using the terms put forward at the outset of this chapter, the Committee diagnosed an imbalance between the processes of differentiation and integration. The Committee recommended that local authorities should adopt a more co-ordinated (that is, 'integrated') approach to the management of local services and put forward proposals for structural reorganization. Before running through these recommendations it is important to understand what it was that the Committee wished to have co-ordinated. To this effect it may be useful to draw upon distinctions, made elsewhere (Greenwood and Stewart, 1973) between three types of local authorities: federal, integral, and separatist. These 'types' are distinguished by their relative pursuit of integration. 'Separatist' authorities are organized on the assumption that the local authority consists of a collection of services each of which may be planned for, and provided, without reference to other services, and which, therefore, require a minimum of co-ordination. 'Federal' local authorities, on the other hand, similarly assume that their functions are largely separate but recognize that a common local authority framework provides opportunities for economies of scale (for example, central purchasing, typing pools, etc). 'Integral' local authorities assume that services are interwoven in their effect upon the community and should be planned as a programme, rather than as an aggregation of activities. In other words, federal authorities pursue essentially *administrative* co-ordination, whereas integral authorities pursue the co-ordination of both administration *and policy.*

There is little doubt that the Committee on Management were pointing to more than mere administrative co-ordination. They were not advising local authorities to 'adopt a 'federal' stance. On the contrary, they had found the need for greater policy co-ordination:

All service departments have close relationships with the Clerk's and treasurer's departments. But many local authority services have little in common; there is no common endeavour in the provision of child care services and the fire services; the weights and measures inspectorate has no contact with the highway engineer; the midwife has more in common with the hospital service outside local government than with the many activities inside the local authority itself. At the same time the separateness and individuality of the various services can be over-emphasised. Many service departments are closely connected. The research report shows clearly the overlap in day-to-day functions between the children's service and health, education and welfare services. In the wider context individual services, however disparate, are provided for the community as a whole. Planning for the development of the community, the allocation of priorities for finance or for space on the drawing board, the timing of the various schemes all demand a co-ordinated approach. [p. 26]

This emphasis upon policy co-ordination (that is, adoption of a view of local authorities as 'integral' rather than 'federal' organizations) ran counter to earlier attempts at co-ordination, which largely centred upon the pursuit of administrative co-ordination. For example, during the 1950s and early 1960s there were a series of experiments designed to achieve what we would refer to as administrative co-ordination. In some instances these experiments quite clearly excluded any element of policy co-ordination. See for example, the changes reported at Coventry (1954).

In other instances the distinction between measures aimed at administrative co-ordination and those aimed at policy, was a rather fine one. Thus, the Principal City Officer appointed in Newcastle is often seen (wrongly) as a precursor of the modern chief executive officer. In fact the purpose of the Harris appointment was to facilitate implementation of the council's redevelopment plans:

> The main functions of the Principal City Officer as laid down were to co-ordinate and organize the council's business, and particularly to be responsible for the implementation of the city's development programme . . . The new officer was expected as well to act as a high-grade progress chaser to ensure that decisions were implemented without delay. [Elliot, 1971, p. 151].

In our terms the emphasis here is on the attainment of administrative co-ordination, rather than upon the integration of policies in their formulative stage. Nevertheless, by the mid-1960s there was an emerging appreciation of the need for local authorities to reconsider the effectiveness of their managerial arrangements. That appreciation found one of its more cogent expressions in the Report of the Committee on Management.

To secure a more adequate balance between the processes of differentiation and of policy integration, local authorities were advised by the Committee on Management to make a number of structural reforms. Some of these were to do with the reduction of differentiation, others to do with the machinery for integration. First, there should be *less* differentiation, that is, fewer committees, sub-committees and departments. No longer should each service be provided through its own committee and department. Instead, 'similar or related functions' should be bundled together, producing at most around six committees and six departments. These numbers contrast markedly with the practices revealed by the Committee's own inquiries which found that in 1964/5 county and county borough councils operated with an average of 'about 20 full committees, between 40 and 50 sub-committees as well as a large number of ad hoc committees and sub-committees' (p. 14). Perhaps the intention of the Committee was to over-emphasize the need for fewer committees and departments. Perhaps the recommendation for only six committees was never seriously thought realistic: the intention might have been to 'shock' local authorities *towards* that number. If that was the case the Committee's strategy was successful, but, as we shall see, that strategy had an unfortunate consequence.

The success of the strategy was that local authorities did not ignore these particular recommendations. All local authorities were prompted to reconsider the adequacy of their committee and departmental structures, and in the substantial majority of cases changes were effected (Greenwood *et al*, 1969). Not that the changes were as radical as those recommended by the Committee — committees and sub-committees were reduced but usually to between ten and fifteen in number: reductions in numbers of departments were rare rather than predominant. Nevertheless, by 1969 the sheer number of organizational 'bits' had substantially fallen in many local authorities, reflecting the influence of the Committee on Management.

The Committee had a second, less deliberate influence on structural differentiation. The Committee's analysis focused almost exclusively upon the excessive numbers of committees, sub-committees, and departments. In this respect their concern was with what we shall refer to as the *extent* of differentiation. This concern is obviously important. But it is not the only aspect of differentiation. Equally interesting and important are questions such as, on what basis should services be grouped together? More particularly, should housing and environmental health be the responsibilities of separate committees, or of one committee? Should the management of libraries, art galleries, museums and other cultural services be linked with educational services, at officer or member level or both, or should they remain separate? Should land-use planning be separated from, or joined with, architectural and/or technical services? And so on. These are questions about the *criteria* of differentiation.

It is unfortunate that the Committee on Management became obsessed with what they regarded as excessive use of committees: by doing so they virtually ignored the question of what services should be linked together and on what basis. There are, it is true, a number of suggestions. For example, *in a footnote*, they suggest that the following six committees might be appropriate in an all-purpose authority:

Planning and development
Housing
Works (including highways and traffic)
Education and culture
Health and welfare
Public protection [p. 44]

Nevertheless, the contribution of the debate within the Committee's report to the question of what is an appropriate criterion of differentiation, is both weak and unfortunate. It is unfortunate because local authorities were misled by the Committee's emphasis and themselves similarly ignored questions of criteria, except in so far that any debate about committee and departmental numbers must brush against the issue of which services should be grouped together or handled separately. Despite the pruning of committee and sub-committee structures there was 'little evidence of any radical redistribution of functions between committees' (Greenwood, Norton and Stewart, 1969). *The important point to be made is that the notion of structural differentiation contains two elements, not one: the extent and the criteria of differentiation. Both of these organizational dimensions form part of our conceptual framework.*

To reduce the extent of differentiation, according to the Committee on Management, would not be sufficient. An adequate balance between differentiation and integration would require the considerable redesign of the existing machinery for integration. It was not sufficient to rely upon 'horizontal committees, personal contacts, party machinery and the efforts of officers to achieve co-ordination' (p. 14). Instead a number of radical steps were necessary. At member level these should include the creation of a management board, with functions that would include the following: 'To formulate the principal objectives of the authority and to present them together with plans to attain them to the Council for consideration and decision . . .' (p. 42). To facilitate this role the management board should be the only executive committee, with all other committees being 'advisory and delibera-tive bodies' except for strictly limited occasions defined for them by the board. At officer level there should be a Clerk, recognized as head of the authority's paid service, and with a responsibility to support the management board.

The responses of local authorities to these recommendations should be considered in two ways. First, we might ask whether the argument for greater *policy* co-ordination was both understood and accepted. Did local authorities appreciate the shift in emphasis set out within the Committee's Report, a shift from administrative to policy co-ordination? Secondly, we might ask whether the particular structural recommendations were accepted. Did local authorities create management boards, chief executive officers, and so forth? The latter question is easier to answer and will be taken first.

At member level the concept of the management board was universally rejected, and strongly condemned. No authority found it convenient or necessary to create a committee with a monopoly of executive authority. Instead, 'The remedy that has been accepted is the constitution of a committee specially charged with those functions (i.e. a general oversight of the council's policies and a greater co-ordination between committees) without the funda-mental alteration in the functions of other committees as proposed by the Maud Committee' (Greenwood, Norton and Stewart, 1969 p. 154). In short, co-ordination was to be achieved by the policy committee. This integrative device was widely adopted, and the debate was less over whether a policy committee was necessary, than what should be its relationship with the majority political party (should minority parties be represented?), and to what extent should it take responsibility for financial matters. These two issues are still debated, and, as we shall see, there is still divergence of practice.

At officer level the idea of a Clerk (as defined by the Committee) was not particularly attractive to local authorities. Shortly following publication of the Committee's views Greenwood *et al.* found that only fourteen county boroughs had recorded any formal decision on the role of the Clerk to bring it in line with the concept of the chief executive officer. Even by 1971 only a minority of authorities had designated their principal chief officer the 'Chief Executive Officer'. It is likely that these figures underestimate the number of authorities in which the town or county clerk exercised responsibilities close to those defined by the Committee on Management. In some cases town or county clerks probably took advantage of the Committee's views to push in the same direction. Thus, in 1971 Greenwood *et al.* reported that a considerable majority of authorities claimed that their clerk (title and terms of reference unchanged) exercised responsibilities for the whole of the Council's activities.

The general response of local authorities to the structures advanced by the Committee on Management, in other words, was one of sympathetic rejection. The details of those structures were not adopted, but, in practice, similar arrangements were usually developed. That is, an increasing number of authorities began to organize themselves to secure greater co-ordination. But, was that to be co-ordination of policy, or of administration? Did local authorities understand and agree in principle with the need for policy co-ordination? The question appears strange, given that structural vehicles such as the policy committee and the chief executive officer were supposed to achieve policy integration. But the important point is that the need for policy co-ordination was largely taken for granted, rather than fully understood and articulated. The reports of local authorities accepted the Committee's diagnosis — that policy co-ordination is required — and moved on rapidly to discuss at much greater length how that co-ordination should be obtained. Should there be a policy committee? What should be its composition? There was very little discussion of whether the Committee was right in its analysis.

Perhaps the lack of debate was brought about by the failure of the Committee itself to point strongly the need for policy co-ordination. There is no doubt that the Committee meant local authorities to pursue such co-ordination, but it is easy to confuse one form of co-ordination (of policy) with that of another (administration). And, given that 'co-ordination' is an emotive word with affirmative associations, it is not surprising that the need for co-ordination was readily accepted. But whether local authorities accepted the need for, and understood the possible implications of, policy co-ordination, is a moot point. One important consequence of this lack of debate was that an increasing number of authorities found themselves structurally geared to a developing conception of policy co-ordination that was not fully approved or intended either by members or officers. This almost accidental introduction of structures for policy integration was to have significant consequences in later years, as we shall note later in our analysis.

In the late 1960s and early 1970s the embryonic notion of policy co-ordination became amplified and developed in the emerging movement for 'corporate planning'. This movement had a number of important effects, not least of which was to switch the attention of local authorities away from an exclusive concern with structural machinery in favour of techniques for policy analysis. These techniques have been documented elsewhere and it is unnecessary to describe them again (Eddison, 1973; Stewart, 1971; Skitt, 1975; Greenwood and Stewart, 1974). What is important is that the ideas of corporate planning had significant implications for matters of organizational design, not least of which was the construction of integrative machinery at the officer level. For example, corporate planning led to the development of the management team of chief officers, a concept which had barely been raised by the Committee on Management. Thus, in 1971 Greenwood, Smith and Stewart wrote that

A concern for administrative efficiency may lead to an emphasis upon the relationship between the principal chief officer and particular chief officers on particular issues and the development of a chief officers' meeting to discuss the use of common services. It is unlikely to lead to any major emphasis on the role of this meeting in the organisation of the authority.

It is only when one moves towards corporate planning that the need to cover the whole range of the affairs of the authority and to involve chief officers in the process of corporate planning gives a new emphasis and a new character to the chief officers' meeting.

> Corporate planning is leading to the concept of corporate management in which at least certain chief officers accept responsibility for the affairs of more than their own department. It is expressed through a chief officers' group which differs from the traditional chief officers' meeting in that it concerns itself not with a limited range of issues but with affairs of the authority as a whole. Such a body was named in the survey a management team. [p. 12]

There were other notable implications for structure, including an increasing use of programme committees (which meant a return to questions of the criteria of differentiation), the creation of corporate planning 'units', and the development of interdepartmental policy groups.

Running through all these developments, however, are two questions of integration, that require separate analytical treatment. Just as there are two elements of differentiation so there are two elements of integration. First, there is the matter of how much integrative machinery is required. This is the notion of volume or extent of integration. A concern with this question would lead to a consideration of whether policy committees, chief executive officers, management teams, or corporate planning units were necessary in any given authority. These are questions to do with the *extent of integration.* Secondly, there is the question of the pattern or style of integration. Will service committees work through the policy committee and have no independent recourse to the full council? Will chief officers be bound by collective decisions of the management team, or will they be expected to voice their dissent in front of members? Will analysis be prepared by interdepartmental teams, or by central specialist units? These are questions to do with the *style of integration.*

The concept of an integrative style is an important one and will figure in later chapters. It is, therefore, of some importance that it is properly understood. It is clarified by contrasting the practices of two authorities in the pre-Reorganization era. These authorities adopted strongly contrasting patterns of structural integration. One authority — Hull — adopted practices close to what we shall term a concentrated style of integration. The other — Coventry — had practices closer to a matrix or deconcentrated style of integration.

At Hull the Council engaged the services of McKinsey and Company Inc. to advise upon the overall management arrangements of the authority. At committee level the primary concern of the consultants was with problems of resource allocation between services that have no obvious common denominator. A hierarchy of choice was proposed; at the highest level the policy committee would allocate broad sums of expenditure between seven services committees, which in turn would allocate resources to the services within their terms of reference. To facilitate this descending process of choice, committees were made responsible for services serving a common objective. For example:

> Recreational services is one example of a programme area, since it brings together all the activities relating to the leisure needs of the public. The programme committee in charge of recreational services would be responsible for determining priorities in that area by assessing the needs of one leisure service against another, say swimming pools against playing fields. The Policy Committee, on the other hand, will be concerned with priorities at a higher level — i.e. assessing one programme area against another, say recreation against education. [McKinsey and Co. Inc., 1971, pp. 2-7]

The consultants found it necessary to allocate responsibilities at the departmental level in a manner consistent with that adopted at member level. For although they admitted that the programme planning concept (the arranging of activities according to objectives in order to facilitate choice) 'applies first and foremost to the organisation of committees', it was felt that

> The same principles should be extended to the organisation of departments, so that committees and departments may be organised in a one-to-one relationship. Such an arrangement will ensure (1) committees receive consistent and coherent advice on the formulation of policy, and (2) the body responsible for policy also has the authority to see that policy is implemented effectively.

The responsibilities of the programme departments were carefully defined in order to remove the duplication of effort that had existed under the previous system 'as a result of poorly defined responsibilities'.

Perhaps the more novel recommendation of the consultants was for an 'Executive Office', which would

> . . . assume the present responsibilities of the Town Clerk's and City Treasurer's Departments, and most of the responsibilities of the Town Planning Department. The Office should also take on the additional functions of corporate planning. Leading the Office should be a triumvirate of officers holding the posts of Town Clerk, City Treasurer and Director for Community Planning. One of these

officers should be designated chief executive and the other two deputies. In addition, an Officer's management group should be set up, composed of the members of the triumvirate plus the heads of the programme directorates and the three support divisions of the executive office. [pp. 2-7]

These structural recommendations imply that the style of integration envisaged by the consultants relied upon the creation of large structures at the centre of the administration pulling together the activities and decisions of the seven programme areas. Analysis would be carried out primarily by specially appointed staff located within the Executive Office, and largely for the benefit of the chief executive and deputy chief executives. Major items of business would be routed through the Executive Office and from there to the policy committee.

The above style of integration contrasts with that built into the structural arrangements of Coventry in the years preceding reorganization. There, the Council operated through thirteen service committees: administration, education, estates and general purposes, finance, general works, housing, international friendship, planning and development, public protection, recreation, social services, transportation and highways, and health. At the centre of these was a policy committee whose terms of reference were drafted 'with the general objective of enabling the Council "to study the physical and social environment of the City as a whole, to assess its future needs and to lay down the major objectives, reconciling one with another and determining their priorities" '.*

Thus, the principal difference between the committee structures of Coventry and Hull is that the former operated without programme committees. Of rather greater interest, however, are the differences at departmental level and it is these that illustrate our main point.

At Coventry *there was no concentration of functions within the department of the chief executive officer.* Instead the chief executive officer operated without departmental responsibilities, except for limited secretarial assistance and the services of a single senior officer. This lack of a central department emphasized the

---

*Quotations referring to Coventry C.B. are from council documents not available for general circulation. References are therefore not given.

position of a 'chief officer's team' composed of senior heads of department which met weekly under the chairmanship of the chief executive officer. This team considered items of policy, prepared advice for the service committees as well as the policy committee, and submitted to the latter recommendations for the annual revenue budget and the capital programme. These formal meetings were supplemented by less structured daily meetings open to all heads of departments, at which officers were expected to 'identify problems likely to arise so that arguments can be made for dealing with them . . . pass on to each other the germs of ideas . . . keep each other informed of (their) movements and . . . clear many of their minor items which require consultation'.

The lack of structural centralization was reflected in the organizational location of three 'resource units' within the separate departments of the city treasurer, city architect and planning officer, and the associate town clerk. These units advised the chief officer's team of 'the demand and availability of their particular type of resources (i.e. finance, land or manpower) not just in the short term of the next year, or even five years, but also in the longer term of up to fifteen years'.

There was no attempt to reduce the number of departments through amalgamation or the appointment of directors. The Council retained the existing range of departments as the basis of their organization, without necessarily accepting that the distribution of responsibilities was correct and would remain unchanged. A network of interdepartmental teams were superimposed *laterally* upon the departmental organization for purposes of co-ordination. These were of two main types — *programme area teams*, responsible for consideration of the impact of existing and alternative courses of action upon the policy objectives of the local authority; and *programme implementation control groups*, responsible for large-scale capital projects that required inter-departmental co-ordination.

These departmental arrangements may be contrasted with those designed for Hull, in order to isolate two aspects of integrative style, one of which will be used in later chapters. These will be labelled the extent of concentration, and the extent of *centralization*. Centralization is to do with *the locus of authority* to take decisions or to act over particular issues. That is, a centralized structure would be one in which the level at which decisions are taken is towards the top of the authority hierarchy: a decentralized structure would have decisions taken towards the bottom of the hierarchy. For example, an authority which allows a chief officer to appoint his own deputy is less centralized than one that requires appointments of this nature to go before a committee of members. Similarly, an authority which allows assistant chief officers, or headteachers, or area organizers in the social services, to exercise virement (that is, the movement of money from one area to another) within the framework of their budgetary provisions, is less centralized than an authority which requires virement to be authorized by the finance or policy committee. These examples illustrate the more usual meaning attached to the idea of centralization.

Centralization, however, is acquiring a 'new' meaning in local government. Sometimes officers and members refer to their authority as centralized and mean that the policy committee, and/or the chief executive 'interfere' with the deliberations of service committees and departments. Thus, a policy committee may exercise the right to comment, but not decide, upon reports prepared by service committees before these committees put recommendations to full council. Reports of the service committees may go 'through' the policy committee to council. This routing and process of consultation and involvement is often referred to as an indication of increasing centralization. Unfortunately, to use the term centralization in this way can be confusing. To avoid confusion we shall distinguish between centralization (the locus of authority to take decisions) and concentration. Concentration is to do with the routing of matters through the local authority, and the involvement of various officers and members. For example, an authority which allows a service committee to receive advice from a service department and to report directly to council would be less concentrated than an authority which requires issues to involve programme area teams and to be routed through the management team and the policy committee. More specifically, individual capital schemes in some authorities are considered by the relevant service department and service committee; in others they go to a corporate group set up to appraise all capital schemes, and then to the management team before individual schemes are submitted to service and policy committees. The former authority is the less concentrated as it involves fewer departments and committees and does not route matters through the integrative structures.

The structures of Hull, as described, are both more centralized and more concentrated than those of Coventry. They demonstrate a concentration of analysis within the executive office and a routing of matters through that office. There is also a centralization of influence within the higher reaches of the authority. Coventry, on the other hand, although exhibiting elements of concentration (for example, corporate group reports are routed through the management team) is *comparatively* less concentrated. Formal hierarchical levels of the authority's structure are criss-crossed with lateral links structured around interdepartmental groups. These groups ensure the involvement of many rather than few service areas in decision making. They pull in the expertise of, and information possessed by, many officers able to contribute to particular issues requiring policy analysis. Diffusion of responsibility for issues is much greater than at Hull, and although any significant issue would ultimately be considered by the policy committee it would do so only after considerable negotiation between various affected service areas. At Hull, responsibility for analysis would be clearly within, and largely restricted to, the executive office. The executive office is the embodiment of a much firmer concentration in the routing of reports and decisions, and restricted involvement over important issues.

These differences are matters of integrative style. On the one hand, Hull is both concentrated and centralized in its approach to policy co-ordination. On the other, Coventry is rather less concentrated and more decentralized. It is important to distinguish between these two aspects of style as they are not necessarily related (see Hinings *et al.,* 1980). Both aspects of style are important and are matters of current concern throughout local government. Here, however, we must restrict our analysis to the notion of concentration. The data obtained through the questionnaire survey of all local authorities was deliberately restricted to the one aspect of integrative style, namely structural concentration. Nevertheless, some discussion of centralization will be woven into the analysis presented below, based upon the study of twenty-seven authorities.

During the early 1970s these differences in style were given an increasingly central place in discussions on structure. At conferences and in local government journals much less emphasis was given to questions of differentiation and rather more to questions of integration, and especially to questions about the appropriate style of integration. A favourite theme became whether or not the chief executive should have departmental responsibilities, who should be on the management team, whether there should be units composed of corporate planning specialists, and, at member level, whether the policy committee should exclude members of minority parties. The contrast with the debate following the report of the (Maud) Committee on Management, during which the important issues were over numbers of committees and departments, whether there should be a chief executive style Clerk, and so forth, is noticeable.

All of these issues, however, had to be considered together, both by the (Bains) Working Group on new management structures and the (Paterson) Advisory Group on management structures for local authorities in Scotland. Both committees sought and received information on the experiences of a range of local authorities and set out their conclusions in the form of structural recommendations. Both committees also paid attention to the four aspects of organizational design identified in the preceding discussion. In this respect their reports are much more balanced than that of the Committee on Management which, as we have seen, neglected aspects of criteria and style. Thus, the Bains Working Group not only recommended that local authorities should keep numbers of sub-committees and committees to a minimum, but went on to consider the grouping of services and functions:

> the evidence suggests to us that . . . groupings have sometimes been made on a rather superficial basis. The groupings require very careful consideration before they are formed and should be capable of being changed . . . [p. 34]

After some discussion the Working Group opted for 'programme committees' as the more likely vehicle for the development of a corporate approach. At departmental level, on the other hand, the Working Group was less convinced of the merits of directorate structures (that is, departments grouped to form programme administrations) and were inclined to prefer the more traditional service departments as the criteria of differentiation.

The various recommendations on programme committees and service departments are important and substantial parts of the

Group's Report, but more attention is placed upon the appropriate form of integrative machinery. The Group felt it necessary to elaborate in detail the need for a policy committee and appropriate sub-committees, a chief executive without departmental responsibilities, and a management team of chief officers supported by a matrix of corporate groups. Indeed, the Group went on to provide draft terms of reference for a policy and resources committee, and a job specification for a chief executive. These details are important because they indicate the strong concern expressed in the Report that local authorities should have both sufficient structures for the purpose of policy co-ordination, and a style of integration that would prove acceptable to officers and members and which would therefore prove workable. Interestingly, the strong commitment of the Working Group to a style of integration at officer level based upon decentralization and deconcentration (as evidenced by a chief executive working through a network of corporate groups headed by a management team of chief officers), a commitment based upon the assumption that a more centralized system would prove unworkable, contrasts sharply with the advice of the Paterson Advisory Group that the larger Scottish local authorities should create an Executive Office:

> We have already indicated that the chief executive should not have direct responsibility for a major department except in the smaller authorities; at the same time, however, it is vital to ensure that he does not become isolated but has at his disposal all the necessary facilities to keep himself fully informed and, in particular, to carry out his co-ordinative role in policy planning. His support will clearly come in large measure from the heads of the service departments and the central support services and from the policy planning unit where it exists.
>
> In the larger authorities, however, the immense demands which will be made on the chief executive require a more formalised arrangement for his support. We favour the concept of the 'executive office' whereby the chief executive is assisted, in his tasks of co-ordinating policy planning, monitoring the effectiveness of the authority's programmes and managing the central services, by two or three officials of chief officer status. These would be a director of finance, a director of administration and, in the largest authorities of all, a director of policy planning. These officers could be designated as deputy chief executives. [pp. 68-70]

Further details of the two reports need not be set down here. The interested reader may refer to them at leisure. Our purpose in briefly reviewing some of the salient recommendations has been to reinforce the point that the recent history of local government demonstrates a recurring concern with the appropriate extent and criteria of differentiation, and with the extent and style of integration. These concepts, summarized in Table 2.1, have emerged over the past fifteen years as the important questions of organizational design. By tracing the changing balance of emphasis during these years, and showing how an initial and overriding concern with the extents of integration and (especially) differentiation has been replaced by a more balanced discussion of all four aspects of organization, we have, hopefully achieved two purposes. First, the conceptual definitions have been sharpened and the distinctions separating the four aspects of organizational design have been clarified. Perhaps more importantly, the review of local government reports serves to remind the reader that the concepts which form the basis of our subsequent analysis are seen as important in and by local government, and have contemporary relevance. The labels may be unfamiliar, but the issues are not. The conceptual framework is not an academic construct divorced from the concerns of the practising councillor and administrator: it is a vehicle for an understanding of those concerns.

TABLE 2.1　*A Conceptual Framework for the Analysis of Local Authority Structures*

Differentiation	
extent	number of organizational parts
criteria	basis of dividing and grouping tasks and responsibilities
Integration	
extent	number of co-ordinating devices
style	relative emphasis upon concentration as a means of securing policy co-ordination

D. N. Chester, reviewing the Report of the Committee on Management, was apprehensive that the strident recommendations would be adopted wholesale: 'there is thus a danger of a new orthodoxy' (1968, p. 296). The advantage of hindsight made Chester's fears ill-founded. Perhaps there was greater call for alarm following publication of the Bains Report. The shadow councils elected in 1973 had to struggle to meet the tight timetable of an imminent reorganization. They might have been forgiven for adopting the Bains proposals without too much thought, given the insufficient time available for systematic consideration of other possibilities. Again, however, such fears would have been at least partly ill-founded. The structural arrangements of local authorities in the post-reorganization years still exhibit important variations. It is the purpose of the next chapter to describe that variation using the four concepts explicated above.

CHAPTER 3

Local Authorities in the
Post-Reorganization Period

INTRODUCTION

The conceptual framework set out in the previous chapter will be used in this and the following chapter to compare the structural practices of local authorities, both as they currently exist and in terms of recent changes. The conceptual framework, as we have stressed, is not an academic construct of relevance only to the student or researcher: it is based upon structural issues underlying the organizational design of local authorities. Thus, both in using the concepts summarized on p. 30 and in examining the structural practices of local authorities, we are, in effect, looking at the responses of local authorities to the questions posed by these underlying structural issues. How many and what type of service committees and departments should be established, how should they be co-ordinated, what should be the balance between service and integrative structures, and how should service and integrative structures interrelate? These are the kinds of issues upon which our conceptual framework is constructed, and the structural practices of local authorities are the responses of local authorities to them.

The practices of local authorities will be summarized in two ways. Initially each structural issue will be considered separately. Thus, we can ask how many committees, sub-committees and departments have been set up: that is, what is the extent of differentiation. We can then ask about the extent of integration and so on. The essential purpose will be to map out the practices of local authorities to show the variations that currently exist throughout local government. A subsidiary purpose, will be to trace shifts in emphasis that have occurred over the past ten to fifteen years. Taking as a starting point 1964-5 (the research year of the Committee on Management) we shall show how the present structures of local government have evolved.

Local authorities of course, do not respond to the issues of structural differentiation and integration as though they are *separate* issues. It may be convenient to dissect and analyse structural practices in this way, but the organizational arrangements of local authorities are a combination of responses to structural issues. Local authorities have to decide on how many and what type of service structures and on how many and what type of integrative structures are needed as if these issues are related. Analytically we may wish to consider them separately: empirically they are bound together. It is rather important, therefore, to examine the *patterns* of organizational design developed by local authorities. We must ask, to what extent are local authorities operating with many service committees and departments also characterized by many integrative structures? Put another way, if a particular authority's response to the process of differentiation is to create many service committees and departments, will the same authority respond to the problem of integration by creating *many* integrative structures. Is there a balance between service differentiation and extent of integration? Answers to this and related questions may be obtained by considering eight possible organizational patterns and assessing their relative popularity. An attempt will also be made to identify operational problems and difficulties that might be experienced with alternative organizational patterns.

This and the next chapter, in other words, are principally concerned with laying out the amount and form of variation that exists in the structural practices of local government. Here the four structural issues are considered separately. In the next chapter they are treated in terms of organizational patterns. Wherever appropriate the recent historical context is presented in order to trace the direction and content of recent trends.

These complementary purposes — the mapping of current variation and the trends of recent years — are handled in rather different ways. There is little difficulty in summarizing variations and similarities in structures. Data from the 1977-8 questionnaire survey, interwoven with illustrations from particular authorities, is sufficient for this purpose. Rather more difficulty occurs in summarizing the main changes that have occurred since 1964. It was noted in Chapter 1 that there are several available studies of local authority structures as they have developed since 1964. Unfortunately, these studies were not conducted in the same way and the details of the published material are not always consistent. For example, in order to know accurately the extent of differentiation data must be available on the combined use of committees, sub-committees and departments in each authority. To know only that many (but not all) authorities have many committees and also that many (but not all) authorities have sub-committees, is not sufficient. It could be that significant numbers of authorities have either many committees or (but not also) many sub-committees, in which case the extent of differentiation at member level would, in general, be less than if many authorities had both many committees and many sub-committees. The researches of the Committee on Management presented its data in the former manner, making it almost impossible to represent accurately the combined structural practices of local authorities. For this reason information concerning changes over time cannot be offered in the same systematic fashion that is employed for the portrayal of inter-authority variation. Nevertheless, reasonable assessments may be made concerning the principal changes that have occurred over the past fourteen years, and we shall have to be content with making best use of the material at our disposal.

EXTENT OF DIFFERENTIATION

All local authorities divide their responsibilities between committees, sub-committees and departments. The volume of work and the complexity of business make it impossible to discharge all responsibilities through the Council and from a single administrative department. Committees and departments are inevitable consequences of local authority size and the magnitude of the Council's responsibilities. What is uncertain is how many committees, sub-committees and departments should be set up. At what point do the advantages of specialization become outweighed by the difficulties of co-ordination? What, in other words, might be an optimum extent of structural differentiation?

Local authorities have always varied in their responses to this question, as will be seen in a moment. Equally interesting, however, is to note the changing fashion that has occurred since 1964-5. At that time, as indicated in Chapter 2, local authorities tended to operate with many committees, sub-committees and departments:

> The Law requiring certain committees to be set up for specific purposes, combined with the practice of establishing a committee for each service of the authority, leads to the setting up of numerous committees. The average number of committees in county councils is 19, and in county borough councils 21. These averages conceal some considerable variations. There may be as few as 12 committees in a county council or as many as 29; the range in county borough councils is between 12 and 35. County and county borough authorities with their wider range of functions have more committees than the other types of authority. But the research report cites the case of a rural district council with a population between 10,000 and 20,000 having 20 committees and a county borough council with a population between 200,000 and 400,000 having only 15.
>
> In the same way as the council in order to deal with the pressure of business and its complexity has fallen back on the creation of committees so committees themselves have created sub-committees. The range in the number of sub-committees is even wider. Urban and rural district councils have very few, and the numbers in non-county borough councils average only nine but the research report cites instances of authorities using 50, 30 and 28 sub-committees. In county borough councils the average number of sub-committees is 40, but the largest number found was 160 and the smallest a mere three. The average number of sub-committees in county authorities is 47, but the range is somewhat less than in county borough councils. Not all of these sub-committees meet either frequently or regularly. The nature of their work varies; the examples quoted in the research report of sub-committees to consider the use of the coat of arms, dry rot in the town hall, the Christmas carol service and the cattle grids suggest that the significance of their work is sometimes limited. Moreover, the limited samples dealt with in the research report do not suggest that the existence of sub-committees results in less pressure on the main committee. [p. 32]

The critical diagnosis of the Committee pushed local authorities into reviewing and reducing their committee structures and, to a lesser extent, their departmental arrangements. The fashion became to have few rather than many organizational parts, irrespective of the difficulties that might be caused. For example, fewer committees made it difficult to provide councillors with interesting and influential roles, but this was not seen to override the possible advantages of co-ordination. The fashion for fewer committees and departments quickly established itself and was reinforced by the argument and recommendations of the Bains Working Group:

> In the years which have elapsed since the Maud Report, many authorities have reduced the overall number of committees. Some have done so in order to slim the administration and encourage co-ordination, some to reduce calls on officers' time, some to help break down departmentalism and others, we fear merely because it was felt to be fashionable to do so. There can be no doubt that a large number of separate committees can present severe problems of co-ordination, particularly when those committees are linked not to the objectives of the Council but to the separate departments through which those objectives must be secured and we would not wish to disagree in any way with the Maud recommendation in this respect. [p. 29]

In effect, the Working Group were advising local authorities to reduce or maintain their committees and departmental structures below the numbers prevalent before Reorganization. They recommended that large local authorities would not require more than six committees, a considerably lower number than that found in most authorities before Reorganization. How far local authorities have found it necessary or advisable to follow the thrust of the Group's recommendations is given in Table 3.1. The table summarizes the number of committees, sub-committees and departments found throughout local government in 1977-8. Before commenting upon the variation depicted by that table two points can be made. The data is presented separately for committees and departments, but there is a strong association between numbers of committees, plus sub-committees, and numbers of departments. That is, an authority with many committees and sub-committees also tends to have many departments. For this reason data is provided on 'overall' differentiation.

The second point is that in one sense comparatively little change has occurred since 1974 in the number of committees and departments. The variation observed in Table 3.1 is similar to that found in 1974: hence there is no need to repeat the data for 1974. But that general conclusion should not conceal movements within the overall pattern.

While the system as a whole has remained stable, considerable

TABLE 3.1   *Extent of Differentiation*

	Shire Districts	Shire Counties	Met. Districts	Met. Counties	London Boroughs
Numbers of Committees and sub-committees					
1-5	8	0	0	0	0
6-10	115	0	1	1	0
11-15	127	2	5	2	6
16-20	43	11	5	3	7
21-25	8	17	8	0	6
26-30	1	11	4	0	4
31+	0	3	11	1	2
Range	Min 3 Max 28	Min 13 Max 43	Min 6 Max 39	Min 7 Max 31	Min 11 Max 40
Numbers of departments					
1-5	66	0	0	0	0
6-10	217	7	13	3	10
11-15	17	29	15	3	12
16-20	1	5	6	1	2
21+					1
Range	Min 2 Max 18	Min 8 Max 16	Min 7 Max 18	Min 7 Max 16	Min 6 Max 24
Overall differentiation, committees, sub-committees and departments					
1-5					
6-10	7	0	0	0	0
11-15	79	0	1	0	0
16-20	119	0	0	1	1
21-25	66	2	3	2	3
26-30	25	6	3	2	7
31-35	5	10	10	1	6
36-40	1	16	5	0	4
41-45	0	7	4	1	2
46-50	0	1	5	0	2
51-55	0	1	2	0	2
56+	0	1	1	0	2
Range	Min 8 Max 36	Min 21 Max 56	Min 13 Max 57	Min 16 Max 45	Min 20 Max 56

change has occurred in individual local authorities, especially in numbers of committees and sub-committees. Nineteen of the twenty-seven authorities experienced some change in committees and sub-committees, although usually of a limited form. In most cases change involved the abolition or addition of one to three committees or sub-committees. Rather less change has occurred at the departmental level, although some changes are under consideration. Thus, although the amount of variation between authorities has not altered since 1974/5, this should not conceal the modest changes occurring in many authorities.

Having made these points it is appropriate to return to the variation between authorities depicted in Table 3.1. Clearly, there is considerable variation throughout local government. Numbers of committees, sub-committees and departments differ from authority to authority. Thus, one shire district authority has a total of eight committees and sub-committees, whereas a second authority has more than three times that number. One metropolitan district has six committees and sub-committees, another has thirty-nine. Similarly, numbers of departments range from an authority with two service departments to one with twenty-four.

A moment ago it was suggested that the amount of variation in 1977/8 (shown in Table 3.1) is close to that of 1974/5. That broad stability may well change in the next few years. Local authorities are currently reviewing and reconsidering the basic principle underlying the Report of the Bains Working Group and substantially incorporated within the structure of most local authorities in 1974/5. That is, several authorities are questioning whether 'the corporate approach' is appropriate. This debate focuses upon the need for various integrative structures such as the chief executive, the management team, the corporate planning unit and so forth. But the removal of such structures might have a spillover effect upon the extent of differentiation. As the pressures for integration decrease, and the advocates of co-ordination are outnumbered or outspoken by those pressing the advantages of specialization, it is possible that existing committees will spawn sub-committees, or have their responsibilities reallocated between two or more different committees. Rather less likely is that departments will be reorganized, although some moves in this direction are being considered. We are here making tentative guesses about the likely rates of differentiation in the next few years. *Some* authorities may increase their extent of member differentiation as a spillover from the reduced emphasis upon policy co-ordination. If this does occur then the range of inter-authority variation, which is already marked, will increase.

CRITERIA OF DIFFERENTIATION

There are various ways by which local authorities could group or separate their responsibilities. One, extensively recommended in recent years, is based upon the idea of programme areas. As noted in Chapter 2, McKinsey and Co. Inc., the Bains Working Group, and the Paterson Advisory Group all advised local authorities to establish *programme* committees (and sometimes departments). This type of committee was presented as much more useful for the promotion of policy co-ordination than the traditional *service* committee. What these reports actually mean by a service committee is not entirely clear, but it appears to imply a committee responsible for a single service and created in response to legal requirements and professional pressures rather than for more explicitly administrative reasons. Thus, in 1967, the Committee on Management traced the growth of many service committees and departments to the accretion of new functions and the growth of professional aspirations:

> Departmental organization should not be dictated by the professional aspirations of officers nor by their ambitions for principal officer status. Efficiency and economy, should be the only criteria. [p. 57]

The concept of a programme committee is much clearer, reflecting an attempt to group services in terms of their broad purpose or aims. The Bains Working Group described a programme committee in the following terms:

> Some authorities who have submitted evidence to us have reorganised their committee system in the light of their overall plan for administering the work of the authority. After considering their main objectives, they have divided their work into spheres of activity, each with its own objectives and programme for meeting those objectives. Committees have been made responsible for each programme and for the allocation of resources within it. The results of course, differ according to the circumstances of each authority. If we take the library service as an example, several authorities have included this with education in an Education (or Educational Services) Committee, whilst others are administering libraries through an Amenities and Recreation Committee. Another example is a protection programme area which includes both fire brigade and the consumer protection services (weights and measures etc.) There

is nothing to prevent one committee dealing successfully with these two apparently diverse services if the idea of programme areas is accepted and we think that a more effective allocation of resources will result. [p. 32]

The programme, and service criteria, are the principal alternatives discussed in the local government literature and were commonly employed before 1974. But at least two other possible criteria exist. An authority could group its responsibilities by *geographical area.* The local community could be divided into a network of geographical areas with responsibility for each area given to separate committees or departments. Examples of this arrangement are given below. Finally, responsibilities could be grouped in terms of the clientele served. Thus, there might be a committee responsibility for the elderly, or gypsies, etc. We will elaborate upon these latter possibilities in a moment.

In 1964-5 the dominant pattern would appear to have been the service committee and service department. It is not entirely clear whether any other types of committee were employed. By 1971 a measure of change had occurred. The programme committee was seen as a means of translating programme budgeting into structural form and was widely discussed, and sometimes implemented, as a basis for committee organization. And, given the considerable interest expressed in programme budgeting during the late 1960s and early 1970s (e.g. Stewart, 1970; Butt, 1972), not surprisingly a proportion of authorities looked seriously at the programme basis of differentiation. Few authorities, however, were entirely convinced that the programme criterion *by itself* was a useful basis for committee and departmental structures. The number of authorities with a full complement of either programme committees or directorates, along the lines of the Hull structure detailed on p. 23, remained small. Much more common was the creation of one or two programme committees alongside the more traditional service committees. At officer level there was some restructuring along programme lines but to a lesser extent than at member level. In other words, by 1971 the majority of local authorities employed two criteria as a basis for differentiation: service and programme.

The Bains Working Group were impressed with the idea of the programme committee, but not with the programme directorate. Authorities were recommended to adopt the programme criteria as a means of grouping services and functions across the full range of their activities. The Group, however, had reservations about directorates.

> We believe that the concept of a director responsible for a number of departments which have been integrated may lead to improved co-ordination and communication between those departments, but we have reservations about directors who are merely co-ordinators of independent functions. There is little point, in our view, in forcing efficiently run departments into illogical groupings merely to provide an even balance of work between one director and another. Some departments, particularly those with a 'staff' rather than a 'line' function may well be more effective if left alone under their own Chief Officer. If, in the result, one is left with directors whose work load/or responsibility is unequal, this difference must be recognized in terms of status and salary. [p. 60]

Consequently, the Working Group were luke-warm in their assessment of directorates. The approach was not, however, dismissed, and local authorities were offered a choice of two structural forms, one based upon the directorate concept, the other not. In fact, the differences between the descriptions offered to the metropolitan districts, and the shire counties, are to do with two areas of work: on the one hand, *technical services* (estates and valuation, planning, architecture, engineering, environmental health) and on the other *education services* (education, amenities and recreation, libraries). The choice offered to shire districts, by and large, focused essentially upon the technical services, although larger local authorities were provided with a chart including an amenities and recreation officer, an officer not shown on the 'average non-metropolitan district' chart. The amenities and recreation choice is of lesser significance in the district than in the shire counties and metropolitan districts, where there are more functions involved, including education. Strangely, when discussing technical services in the districts, the Bains Study Group posed the choice as integration or separation of engineering, architecture, estates and valuation, but *not* (as was the case in the shire counties and metropolitan districts) of planning. Apart from technical and educational services, authorities of the same type were recommended to have the same sets of departments. For example, the metropolitan districts were each advised to set up directors of housing, of finance, of social services, and of administration.

These recommendations were only partly accepted by local

authorities. Few authorities found it appropriate to use programme committees across the full range of services. On the contrary, the overwhelming majority of authorities preferred, and still use, a combination of service and programme committees, although the number of each type varied between authorities. There was, and still is, much greater acceptance of the Group's idea that directorates were unnecessary. The traditional service department was widely retained, and is still the dominant type of department. The fully-fledged programme structure, in short, is rare at officer or member level. Much more common is the use of service and programme criteria. In this respect there is comparatively *little* variation between authorites.

The absence of variation in the criteria of differentiation employed throughout local government should not obscure the interesting minority of authorities experimenting with rather different forms of organization. Thus, a number of authorities have taken up the idea of area-based committees and departments, over-laying the main committee and departmental structure. At Stockport, for example, the Council operates with six area sub-committees whose functions may be distilled from the following:

> The size of the new authority will make it impossible for every elected member to be familiar with many of its areas and their problems. Nevertheless those problems will continue to exist and it is important that the elected member should be provided with a forum through which he can plead a case on behalf of his constituents. It will also be important to create a community forum through which the community councils, tenants' associations and other pressure groups can voice their demands formally to the local authority. Assuming that within the area of the Metropolitan District Council there are no successor or parish councils, the means to achieve this is the creation of eight area committees, based on ward boundaries, each covering two or three wards of this authority . . .
>
> At the same time several of the service committees — Social Services, Housing, Environmental Health and Control, Recreation and Culture, and Transportation and Works will need sub-committees adequately to deal with the needs of their service. Because, the general public and, indeed, members do not structure their complaints in terms of local authority committees and services, but rather in terms of the problems as they appear to them, it will make for a much more intelligible system if the eight common area committees serve all service committees, in effect as joint sub-committees. This will enable the area committee to make direct recommendations to the service committees which, if approved by

them, will become substantive decisions of the council in the same way as the recommendations of a normal sub-committee. At the same time the area joint committees can have a consultative and advisory role so far as other central functions are concerned, e.g. local plans, slum clearance, educational proposals, and will be the channel through which public participation is achieved, coordinating response from their areas to major service proposals of central committees. They will be a forum for members to air complaints, meet tenants' associations, community councils and local organisations.

They will ensure that the Metropolitan District Council is kept aware of feeling in the district and will prevent the large authority from seeming remote, ensuring its responsiveness to local needs and demands. They will complement the constituency role of members and will enable a member who is perhaps on only one service committee to continue to take a positive interest in the whole of the authority's services as they affect his constituency.

Creation of area committees will ensure that the interests of the outlying districts of the new authority are not forgotten and that the elected member is kept in touch with grass roots opinion. (Council document)

Similar experiments at the officer level are rather less common. Admittedly, a significant proportion of authorities have departments operating with common divisional boundaries, but the departments themselves are service or programme departments. An unusual alternative is found in West Norfolk D.C. where the administration is based upon four area directorates (Figure 3.1).

The idea of area-based committees and departments is not new to local government. Page (1936) refers to an area committee in Manchester that existed almost forty years ago. By the late 1960s however, and in the years preceding the 1974 Reorganization, their usage was of minor significance. Since that time, there has been much more discussion about the need to reconsider area-based arrangements or areal forms of analysis (Webster and Stewart, 1974) and recent years have seen a growing interest and initiative in this form of organisation.

Mason (1978) has identified three antecedents to this growing interest. One important antecedent was the traditional concern amongst social and political theorists with the need to make large-scale public bureaucracies sensitive and responsive to local circumstances and opinion. During the 1960s this concern found expression in the Report of the Committee on Management, and

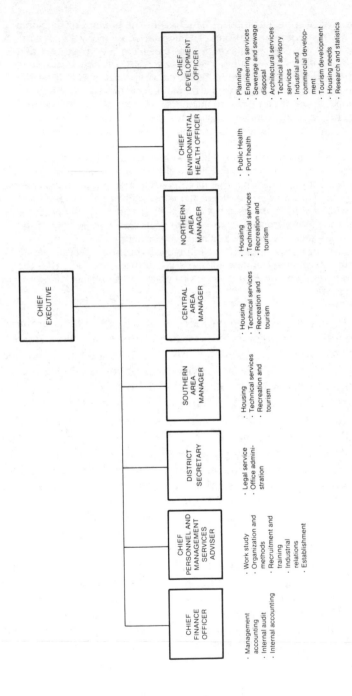

FIGURE 3.1 Area-based departmental structure,
West Norfolk District Council.

in the Royal Commission Report on *Local Government in England 1966-1969* (1969). The Commission put forward the idea of mini-townhalls, and raised the possibility of greater delegation of authority to area-based officers. A second antecedent was the increasing interest in using area-based approaches to tackle the intransigent problems of particular areas: thus analysis and administration is a preparatory step towards 'positive discrimination' in favour of disadvantaged locations. Thirdly, there has been interest in the applicability of area organization as a vehicle for the corporate approach. Some authorities saw area committees and administrative agencies as a vehicle for the promotion of co-ordinated planning and implementation of policies:

> There has been a concern to achieve great sensitivity and responsiveness in the services that local government provides and in its political representation, to concentrate available resources where they are most needed and to extend the co-ordination and corporate planning of services and policies to a local level. [Mason, 1978, p. 6]

We shall note in the next section that the commitment of local authorities to the corporate approach is waning. There is much more disagreement over the applicability of corporate structures and approaches such as those summarized by Stewart (1971) and recommended by the Bains Working Group. As a result certain structures (such as the management team and the chief executive) are under some reconsideration. Interest in area management, on the other hand, shows little evidence of declining. On the contrary, there are probably more authorities now with some form of area organization than was the case in 1974. Area systems of management and organization are becoming increasingly attractive to local government, and also to central government (for example, a number of initiatives aimed at revitalizing the inner cities incorporate aspects of area analysis and administration). In other words, the use of the area criterion of differentiation may well show an increase in the next few years.

A similar conclusion can be reached concerning the fourth criterion — the clientele served. It will be remembered that the Bains Working Group advised local authorities to adopt matrix forms of organization, which, the Group believed, would retain the advantages of service specialization whilst at the same time creating the opportunity for interdepartmental analysis and co-ordination. It was through a network of interdepartmental groups that authorities would overcome the worse excesses of 'departmentalism' and thus achieve a more 'corporate approach'. The Working Group made little comment upon the form that these interdepartmental groups should take, or the way that they should operate. Following Reorganization in 1974 a substantial proportion of local authorities created interdepartmental groups based upon the programme concept. That is, they used the programme criteria of differentiation. Thus, the West Midlands Metropolitan Council had the following:

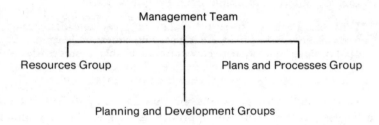

Management Team

Resources Group   Plans and Processes Group

Planning and Development Groups

- transportation
- public protection
- environment
- economic

FIGURE 3.2   Programme-based corporate group structure,
West Midlands County Council (1975).

This network of 'corporate groups', or 'programme area teams' as they were termed in some authorities, was not particularly unusual. Indeed, it corresponded in broad terms to the kinds of arrangements found in many other authorities in the months immediately following Reorganization, reflecting a concern to secure a comprehensive approach to the planning of local services. Unforeseen events, however, served to make these arrangements difficult to operate. Pressures upon resources and the limited recruitment of personnel combined to create conditions hardly conducive for the operation of several groups composed of *senior* personnel discussing essentially *longer-term* issues. There was a feeling that departments could not afford to release staff for corporate group activities, especially as the circumstances surrounding the immediate operation of local government were sufficiently uncertain, and vulnerable to such sharp fluctuations and dislocation, as to make long-term planning an apparently unreasonable aspiration. There was, moreover, a growing disillusionment with the idea of *comprehensive* corporate planning.

As a result of these changing and largely unforeseen events local authorities changed their approach to the design and use of interdepartmental groups. In some instances these groups were disbanded altogether. Elsewhere the number of groups was cut and the attempt at comprehensive planning abandoned. Instead, local authorities began to identify 'key issues' for analysis. This switch from comprehensive to key-issue analysis* has often been accompanied by the creation of groups organized in terms of the clientele served. Once the local authority drops the initial focus upon broad, long-term aims and objectives it becomes easier to consider the creation of groups to study the problems of pre-school children, or the elderly, or immigrants. And, a number of authorities have begun to pursue this course of development. An increasing (if minority) proportion of authorities are creating groups to look at 'the total needs of, and provisions for the elderly', or 'the requirements of the under-fives'. These experiments may well increase as authorities are forced to abandon comprehensive approaches to policy analysis and co-ordination.

The use of clientele and area criteria of differentiation are exceptions rather than the general practice. Their potential importance is evident and we have suggested that the incidence of area and clientele based committees and groups might well increase. In 1977-8 the considerable majority of local authorities operated with a combination of service and programme criteria. There have been interesting experiments in the years following Reorganization, both with area forms of organization, and with groups focused upon specific clientele. These, however, remain minority, if significant initiatives.

*This switch is discussed further under the section dealing with style of integration, pp. 57—65.

EXTENT OF INTEGRATION

In 1967 the Committee on Management of Local Government criticized the lack of appropriate arrangements for the co-ordination of policymaking. Local authorities lacked effective arrangements at officer level to provide integrated policy advice, and at member level there was no appropriate means for the debate and determination of policy in co-ordinated form. The framing of policy lacked coherence and consistence. Thus the Committee put forward structural proposals that would overcome these deficiencies. All this, of course, was outlined in the previous chapter. What is of interest here is that the specific structural recommendations of the Committee, taken together, now appear comparatively modest even though at the time they caused widespread disagreement throughout local government. The Committee recommended employment of a chief-executive-style Clerk, who would be at the head of a central department responsible to a 'management board' of members. These would not, of course, have been the only co-ordinating structures. For example, the finance department and committee already existed, and would be retained. There would also be a need for new procedures, linking service committees and service departments with the management board and Clerk. But, in terms of structural units the Committee was unambiguous: the management board and the restyled clerk would be the *only* new units required. Policy co-ordination could be secured substantially through these *two* structures. The Committee did not envisage a substantial increase in the extent (machinery) of structural integration. It is in this sense that we can regard the Committee's proposals as modest.

Despite the modesty of the Committee's proposals they proved difficult for some local authorities to accept. The chief executive concept in particular was an issue of some debate and disagree-ment. As was noted on p. 20, the majority of the larger local authorities operated without a formal chief executive at least until 1971. The idea of a central policy committee was rather more easily adopted although without a monopoly of executive authority. The responsibility of the newly instituted policy committee was usually couched in terms of an advisory rather than instructive role. That is, local authorities were careful to circumscribe the role and influence of the policy committee, rather than, as had been the Committee on Management approach, to curtail the powers of the service committee.

The policy committees established after 1967 may not have had the monopoly of executive authority preferred by the Committee on Management, but they did represent a step towards policy co-ordination. Moreover, the idea of a policy committee became well established in the next few years, and in some authorities began to perform a significant and influential role. Perhaps inevitably the majority of plicy committees concentrated their attention upon the control of policy through the revenue and capital programmes: rather fewer policy committees used the development plan or other, newer forms of planning as their principal tools of analysis and control.

Whatever the limitations of the policy committees in operation, and of the chief-executive-style Clerk, the most significant feature is that from 1967 to 1974 an increasing number of authorities set them up. They became part of the orthodox local authority structures. Interestingly, however, these structures were limited in extent. That is, the majority of local authorities had *few* committees, departments and units principally responsible for the co-ordination of policy. There might be a policy committee, with or without a separate finance committee,* and perhaps sub-committees or full committees for personnel and general purposes. There might be a chief executive, with or without a department, a management team composed of chief officers, and directors of finance, and of legal services, *but there would be little else.* In our terms the extent of structural integration was low. The principal characteristic of the years 1967-74 was a growing introduction of a *restricted* range of particular co-ordinating structures.

---

*The question of whether a policy committee should exist at all, was much less controversial than two related issues concerning what it should do, and how it should be composed. In particular, there was divergence of opinion over whether the policy committee should include responsibility for financial matters. (The arguments for and against this arrangement are succinctly stated by Urwick, Orr and Partners, 1972). The debate on membership was whether minority parties should be excluded, making the policy committee a one-party committee. (The arguments on this are reviewed by the Bains Study Group). These issues were not unrelated, with those authorities preferring a one-party policy committee tending towards the setting up of separate finance committees.

There were exceptions to the trend. A number of authorities pushed the development of co-ordinating structures much further. Thus, corporate planning units, research and intelligence units, programme area teams, resource sub-committees of the policy committee, area sub-committees and the like began to appear. Not all of these devices would be found together. But several of them could be found in various authorities. These authorities were influential in the dissemination of ideas about the form and structures of corporate planning. And, as the ideas of corporate planning became more widely accepted an increasing number of authorities adopted the procedures and structures developed elsewhere. Thus, a second characteristic of the pre-Reorganization period was the growing proportion of authorities experimenting with, or thinking about, the use of greater numbers of separate structures for the pursuit of policy co-ordination. By 1974 the modest ideas of the Committee on Management, which in 1967 had proved difficult to accept, were regarded as insufficient.

The report of the Bains Study Group accelerated this process of emulation by publishing and applauding the development of extensive integrative arrangements. As a result, local authorities generally (we will turn to the exceptions in a moment) now operate with more integrative structures than did authorities before Reorganization. The majority of local authorities have a policy committee (95 per cent) and usually at least two or three sub-committees with responsibility for land (41 per cent), personnel (57 per cent), and aspects of finance (47 per cent). There might also be a sub-committee for performance review (39 per cent) although the precise role of that sub-committee is often uncertain and difficult to identify. There is (still) almost always a chief executive (98 per cent) sometimes with but frequently without (26 per cent) immediate departmental support, although the content of that support varies widely. There is almost always a management team of chief officers (98 per cent), usually at the head of a network of corporate groups (at least 76 per cent have such groups). There are frequently special units for functions such as corporate planning (68 per cent), personnel (86 per cent), management services (77 per cent), and research and intelligence (39 per cent). The net effect is that the extent of structural integration in 1977-8 was noticeably higher than that of 1967-74.

The high incidence of these integrative structures should not conceal the differences found between authorities. Having drawn the main lines of development that occurred between 1967 and 1974 we should beware of assuming that all authorities now look alike. On the contrary, authorities do not have the same combination of integrative structures. That is, although authorities in general have additional structures to those in use before Reorganization, some authorities employ rather more than do others. This is illustrated by Table 3.2. The table summarizes the use of three different types of integrative device. They are:

(1) committees and sub-committees whose responsibilities are directed towards achieving policy co-ordination,
(2) interdepartmental corporate groups (excluding the management team of chief officers),
(3) functional specialisms, officers and units with specific responsibilities for authority-wide co-ordination of key managerial functions such as personnel, finance, policy analysis and research and intelligence.

The table shows clearly significant differences of practice throughout local government. The numbers of co-ordinating committees and sub-committees may be as many as ten, or as few as three. Similarly, the number of interdepartmental corporate groups may be as many as ten, or be limited to the management team. Numbers of functional specialisms range from a minimum of one to as many as eleven. Taking these figures together produces scores for 'overall integration' and indicates an interesting difference between shire authorities, and those of the metropolitan areas (including London). In the shire areas the extreme positions are further apart. Thus, one extreme may be depicted as an authority with only one or (at most) two policy and resource committees and sub-committees, assisted by a chief executive officer at the head of a management team, and by a limited number of functional specialists such as the treasurer, and the director of administration, or secretary. Numerically, such an authority has only nine integrative structures. At the other extreme are authorities with several policy committees and sub-committees, advised and assisted by a full range of functional specialists, and by a chief executive as head of a network of interdepartmental corporate groups drawn together through the management team.

TABLE 3.2   Extent of Structural Integration

	Shire Districts	Shire Counties	Met. Districts	Met. Counties	London Boroughs
Numbers of co-ordinating committees and sub-committees					
1−3	121	5	3	1	6
4−6	167	36	22	5	18
7−9	13	3	7	1	1
10+	1	0	2	0	0
Range	Min 1	Min 1	Min 3	Min 3	Min 2
	Max 10	Max 7	Max 10	Max 9	Max 8
Numbers of interdepartmental corporate groups					
0	91	2	2	1	3
1−3	151	25	14	3	8
4−6	51	12	16	3	9
7−9	8	5	2	0	4
10+	1	0	0	0	1
Range	Min 1	Min 1	Min 1	Min 0	Min 0
	Max 10	Max 9	Max 8	Max 6	Max 11
Numbers of functional specialisms					
0−2	121	2	8	0	6
3−5	175	41	23	5	17
6+	5	1	3	2	2
Range	Min 1	Min 2	Min 2	Min 3	Min 2
	Max 6	Max 6	Max 6	Max 7	Max 11
Overall integration					
6−10	1	1	0	0	0
11−15	42	0	0	1	2
16−20	221	35	16	4	13
21−25	38	18	17	1	10
26−30	0	0	1	1	0
Range	Min 9	Min 9	Min 17	Min 15	Min 14
	Max 25	Max 25	Max 27	Max 26	Max 24

Numerically such an authority has as many as twenty-five integrative structures. Outside of the shire areas the former type of authority is not found. The minimum number of integrative structures in the metropolitan areas is fourteen, whereas the maximum figure is similar to that of the shire authorities. In other words, metropolitan authorities as a group have been much more influenced by the movement towards greater integration than have the shire authorities. Why this is the case will be considered in later chapters.

The difference between local authorities indicated by Table 3.2 are not insignificant. They are less, however, than might have been expected had the Bains Working Group not been set up. It was suggested above that in the years running up to Reorganization there was a growing emulation of those authorities operating with several integrative structures. The widespread credence of corporate planning prompted many local authorities to investigate the possibility of adding to their modest array of integrative structures. This explanation, however, although distinctive of 1971-4, was in no sense a universal process. Not all authorities were equally convinced of the need for those structures and, even if they were convinced, were not disposed at that time to introduce them at once. The process of emulation was largely a gradual if growing diffusion of ideas. The effect of the Bains Working Group was to crystallize and accelerate that process. The Group adopted both the aims (that is, the corporate approach) and many of the structural means of those authorities with high extents of structural integration. The Group gave those aims and structures an official stamp of approval, and recommended them to all local authorities. Not surprisingly, given the pressures of time, most authorities followed the principal ideas and advice within the Group's Report. The Working Group thus catalysed the process of emulation, and turned the evolving trend into a rather sudden, and probably in many cases a hasty acceptance of what were previously minority practices.

Partly the sudden and hasty acceptance of the recommendations put forward by the Bains Working Group is a contributory cause of the dissatisfaction being expressed with existing structures, and of the change in emphasis within the whole debate on local authority organization. Since 1974 local government has witnessed a fundamental reordering of the agenda on organizational structures. The issues now exercising local authorities and creating divided responses are different from those that seemed important in 1973 and 1974. Then, much debate focused upon the organizational position and requirements of the chief executive. Should he have a department and, if so, what should it contain? What form of management team, with what composition and agenda, would provide appropriate support? Similarly, there was debate concerning the relationship between matters of finance and of policy, and disagreement over whether those functions should be combined within the remit of the policy committee. These and similar issues were high on the organizational agenda of 1974. They are issues that are still discussed. But they have been superseded by other, more fundamental, issues. The current debate is less concerned with the details of integrative structures than with the basic aim embodied throughout those structures. That is, there is a questioning of the principles of corporate planning and thus, by inference, of the need for formal policy co-ordination. In some instances the criticisms are expressed as formal council policy (see the extract from Birmingham at the beginning of chapter 5). In others they are expressed as the views of individuals or particular services.

Criticisms of 'the corporate approach' are not typical of *all* authorities. But they are symptomatic of a dissatisfaction in some authorities with that idea. As a result a number of authorities have begun to retreat from the structures established in 1974. Hinings *et al.* (1979a) have identified two sources of retreat: those which are politically inspired, and managerial retreats. Politically inspired retreats from corporate management tended to follow the success of Conservative parties in the 1976 district elections and the 1977 county elections. A significant number of the new Conservative councillors had manifestos which emphasized cutting back expenditure, getting value for money; they identified top-heavy administrations as a problem. Particularly under question were the chief executive, the numbers of chief officers, the role of the management team, and the proliferation of corporate groups. The attack on the corporate structure involved the disbanding of certain organizational arrangements. In a number of cases the management team of chief officers has been disbanded under the direction of members. The reason most usually put forward is that of economy, the management team being identified as a time-wasting body dealing with trivia. If they do not have to attend such a body chief officers can give their attention to their proper duties, namely running their departments. There is a rather more hidden reason, also, for the attack on the management team. Members see it as a body which is too powerful and which usurps the policy-making functions of members.

Hand in hand with the questioning of the management team goes a similar questioning of the need for a chief executive. There have, of course, been a number of well-advertised dismissals of chief executives at Birmingham, North Devon and Exeter (Lomer, 1977). But apart from redundancies, there are changes in the functions of chief executives, sometimes without a change of title. The person remains, the office changes. Thus, chief executives have been taking on day-to-day managerial responsibilities, particularly those of legal and committee administration. In effect the chief executive in such local authorities has returned to the role of clerk, something which is recognized, for example, in Cumbria County Council. Here the chief executive has taken over responsibility for the secretary's department and taken on the title of County Clerk with 'the subsidiary title of chief executive'. In the Birmingham case, not only has the chief executive been made redundant and the management team disbanded, but other organizational sections such as corporate planning and research and intelligence have been disbanded.

Apart from the emphasis on the values of efficiency which inform such actions there is also a genuine desire to return to the known systems of pre-Reorganization days, away from ill-understood, ill-explained and ill-digested systems of corporate planning and management. From the point of view of members the corporate system is often seen as something which not only gives too much power to officers, but is also a system which confuses lines of responsibility and accountability.

Managerial retreats stem from the demand by officers not members for a rethinking of the organizational system. It is impossible to ignore the ideas to which local government officers are subject from a variety of sources such as their professional associations, local government journals and conferences. During the past 18 months there has been an increasing wave of criticism of corporate management. Whereas in 1972-3, when the new structures of local government were being designed, there were no voices raised against the prevailing orthodoxy of corporate management, this acceptance was certainly not the case in 1977-8. What was conventional wisdom three or four years ago has become subject to increasing direction. Thus, the environment of ideas for each authority is much less supportive of the structural entities introduced under the banner of Bains.

Such an environment of critical discussion links up with internal value systems and interests. It allows and encourages those groups whose commitment to corporate planning has never been high to voice their concerns. It is, perhaps, most common in the education service, the highways service and to a lesser extent among librarians (Rowan, 1977; Fiske, 1975; Hansard, 1976). With their traditional autonomy, education officers have often seen themselves as having the most to lose under corporate systems under which power often shifts away from the individual service to chief executives, management teams and corporate groups. Faced with the need to make cuts, the departmentally orientated chief officer returns quickly to the protection of his service against the 'uninformed' judgments of non-professionals in other services. In a time of constraint, according to these critics, it is necessary to cast aside time-wasting activities inherent in corporate working and go back to the certitudes of departmental management. Corporate management becomes the scapegoat for the current ills of the local government world. The difficulties can only be satisfactorily dealt with by dismantling the corporate system and reinstating the autonomy and centrality of the service departments.

The results are similar to those created by the political retreat, it is just the originating point that is different. Chief executives become clerks and take over responsibilities for the administrative and legal functions. Officers meet less regularly or not at all as a corporate entity; the chairman/chief officer/service committee focus is re-emphasized. Power over policy issues rests with the chief officer, and over budgetary matters with the treasurer.

Discussions over the relevance of corporate structure are important because they may well lead to an increasing divergence of practice throughout local government. Fewer authorities can be expected to retain the full range of corporate structures introduced in the initial flush of post-Reorganization enthusiasm. More authorities may dispense with the formal chief executive officer. The management team may wither into disuse. The policy committee may become the traditional finance and general purposes committee, divesting itself of all pretensions to policy co-ordination. Interdepartmental corporate groups will be largely disbanded, and central staffs will be dissipated through service departments. How many authorities will move in this direction is not clear. Hinings *et al.* (1979a) have estimated that the retreat from corporate management over the past four years is characteristic of nine of the twenty-seven authorities within their study. This proportion may well change. What is rather more clear is that despite the number of authorities abandoning corporate structures there are more attempting to make such structures work. These latter authorities may well not retain existing structures in their present form — indeed, in the next section we shall relate some of the significant changes that have occurred already — but we can expect these authorities to exhibit organizational arrangements that contrast markedly with those of authorities dissatisfied with the corporate approach. The contrast will reveal itself in the extent to which authorities utilise integrative structures. In other words, we can expect the variation indicated in table 4.1 to continue and perhaps increase, rather than lessen.

STYLE OF INTEGRATION: EXTENT OF CONCENTRATION

The idea of concentration, as already noted, has to do with the interactions between service committees and departments on the one hand, and various integrative structures on the other. Do service committees always report to, or through, the policy committee? Do service departments have to go through the network of corporate groups headed by the management team of chief officers? These are questions to do with the pattern of interactions. Answers to these questions will also tell something of the pattern of involvement. Where the service committee receives advice from a permanent structure of corporate groups various service areas will have had the chance to comment and contribute upon a policy issue. If the service committee receives advice directly from a service chief officer there is less chance that other service areas will be involved. Similarly, the chief executive who relies upon specialist staff within his department to sift and analyse reports coming from service departments is restricting the pattern of involvement: service departments are excluded from direct participation. Thus, in discussing structural *concentration* we are touching upon the pattern of interactions (how far policy items are fed through the integrative structures) and the pattern of involvement (how far the integrative structures build in the participation of service areas).

Concentration is not an easy concept to handle. Compared to the structural concepts discussed earlier in this chapter, it suffers two disadvantages. First, it is difficult to measure; and secondly there is a lack of coherent material about the practices that existed before 1974.

The problem of measurement may be easily illustrated. During the detailed study of the twenty-seven local authorities an analysis was pursued of the interactions between service and policy committees. Relatively accurate maps were obtained of the frequency of interaction, the subject or purpose of interaction, and the relationship involved in that interaction (that is, what was the authority of the policy committee). Three categories were identified, each found in a number of authorities: the 'co-ordinating policy committee', the 'commenting policy committee' and the 'interventionist policy committee'. The policy and resources (P & R) committee as co-ordinator was found in a small number of authorities. In many ways it can be seen as a natural successor to the pre-Reorganization finance and general purposes committee. The emphasis is on the service committees as producers of policies and programmes with the subsequent need for a committee that can examine the resource implications of such policies. This role may be reflected in the move away from the title 'Policy and Resources' by local authorities in this group to titles such as 'Co-ordinating', 'Resource Planning', and 'Management and Finance'.

The typical situation here is that the service committees report direct to council and it is relatively unusual for the policy committee to report independently. Indeed it may not always be possible for it to do so constitutionally. As one officer said 'the committee is not an overlord and it is definitely not supposed to get in the way of the service committee'. Thus the service committees get their policies approved at the level of council and then the matter is referred to the policy and resources committee to look at the provision of resources for the activity.

With a co-ordination orientated P & R committee one finds that the operation of the committee is very much in the hands of the chief executive, treasurer and secretary. Other chief officers will often be in a position of attending as necessary for particular items. The agenda will come from the secretary and/or the chief executive. It may be the case that the agenda of the P & R committee is made up of a report from each of three central officers. There may also be a regular report from the personnel officer. With a function of co-ordination and resource allocation the role of other chief officers is to present their particular cases, not to be there as members of a management team dealing with overall policy.

The 'commenting policy committee' was the more common form. While the locus of policy-making is still with the service committee, the policy committee has a somewhat more forceful, stronger place in the policy making process of the local authority. None of the authorities in this category have a title for their committee which does not include the word 'policy'. The terms of reference of such committees tend to emphasize policy, not just resources: for example, 'Any committee when entering upon the consideration of any new policy or variation or an existing policy or substantial development shall prepare a report thereon for consideration by the Policy Committee. The Policy Committee shall submit the report to the Council with their observations on the proposals contained therein' (Council document).

Typically in the terms of reference of committees a distinction is made between ongoing activities and new policies, major policies, innovations etc. The policy committee in this situation has the right to comment on *new* aspects of service committee business. This is done through a variety of means. As in the terms of reference quoted above, the onus may be on the service committee to identify items which need to go to the policy committee. But it may be the case that all minutes of all committees go to the policy committee which selects the matters it wishes to comment on. Another possibility is that the chief executive or the secretary vets proposals going to committees. Whatever the system the nub is that the policy committee has the right to make comments on either the policy or resource implications of what the service committee is doing. If it wishes it can recommend to council that the report in question should not be accepted but sent back for further consideration. Thus, typically in this system the reports of policy go to council concurrently with those of the service committee.

The third type of policy committee is more interventionist and 'structuring' in character (by structuring is meant laying down a framework for the operation of the policy process of the authority). Here the policy-making locus will be much more with the policy committee; the policy committee will produce its own ideas, send things back to service committees, direct them in their behaviour. None of the authorities in this group have separated off resource allocation committees as full committees although all of them have some form of sub-committee structure for dealing with detail or working up the policy reports for the full committee. Two particular aspects of the operation of such policy committees stand out. One is the ability to send back reports of service committees before they get to council. In this sense the policy committee is something of an overlord, inter-posing itself between the service committee and the council. Reports and minutes go to P & R before they reach council. The second feature is the extent to which the committee sees itself as being in charge of the corporate plan of the local authority. For example, in one authority, the policy committee has a system of sub-committees responsible for the production of policy recommendations on specific service areas. They report to the policy committee which then gives overall resource targets to the service committees. Thus, the service committees are essentially implementation bodies.

These three types of policy committee, with their different styles of integration, were identified from the study of twenty-seven authorities. Similar differences can be found in the style adopted by the chief executive and the management team. It is not possible, however, to obtain information that would enable us to classify all local authorities in terms of this typology solely through use of a questionnaire. An accurate account of local authority interactions requires the kind of prolonged and intensive analysis only possible with smaller samples. Thus, the questionnaire survey had to rely upon indirect measures. That is, it asked questions about structural characteristics which, on the basis of our understanding of the twenty-seven authorities, provided a reasonable approximation of structural concentration. Thus, a concentrated local authority would have the following characteristics:

1.   A single policy committee, with few if any sub-committees and an absence of other full committees charged with aspects of policy or resource co-ordination. All facets of policy co-ordination are woven together within the terms of reference of this single committee: there is no attempt to fragment responsibility for co-ordination between several committees. This arrangement is

frequently associated with an insistence that service committees refer matters to the policy committee before they go to full council. The smaller the number of co-ordinating committees and sub-committees, the more concentrated is the local authority.

2. The policy committee will be limited to members of the majority party. The widespread practice of including members of other parties is not found within the concentrated authority. The political party is locked into the formal apparatus of the local authority, enabling the senior politicians of the majority party to debate and decide significant and key issues with the assistance of chief officers. They are thus fully informed of likely consequences. The more parties involved on the policy committee, the less concentrated is the authority.

3. The status of the policy committee is emphasized through the attendance of all chief officers on the management team. The management team may not (and usually will not) be composed of all chief officers. In the 'concentrated' local authority only the senior chief officers are members of the team. It is these chief officers who attend the policy committee. This reinforces the relationship between the principal integrative structure at officer level (the management team) and that at member level (the policy committee). In doing this, the link between service chief officer and service committees is downgraded. A concentrated authority has a policy committee regularly attended by the full management team.

4. The chief executive will operate with an extensive department, usually incorporating sections responsible for policy analysis and corporate planning, research and intelligence, management services, and perhaps the personnel function. These functions, if not directly within the chief executive's department, will operate in a 'special relationship'. The intention is that considerable analysis and report preparation will be done by these specialized staffs, rather than by officers seconded part-time from the service departments. The greater the number of functions within the chief executive's department, the more concentrated the authority.

5. There will be a small management team. The involvement of all chief officers is seen as neither necessary nor important. The chief executive relies upon his own staff for execution of policy analysis, and upon the small management team for political support and commitment at officer level. The smaller the proportion of

chief officers on the management team the more concentrated the local authority.

6.   There are few, if any, interdepartmental corporate groups. Policy analysis and review is the function of the chief executive's department. Corporate groups are limited in number and their terms of reference carefully circumscribed. Where they exist they will include a representative of the chief executive's department, who may well act as chairman and take responsibility for the drafting of reports. Not all service departments will be represented. The fewer the number of corporate groups the more concentrated is the local authority.

Authorities vary in their combinations of these aspects of structural concentration. By ignoring these differences however, authorities can be classified in terms of their *extent* of structural concentration. Table 3.3 shows how many authorities have highly concentrated structures, how many have low structural concentration, and so on.

TABLE 3.3   Extent of Structural Concentration

	Number of Authorities								
Extent of Concentration	Shire Counties		Shire Districts		Met. Counties		Met. Districts		London Boroughs	
18—23 highly de-concentrated	2	5%	13	4%	1	14%	7	21%	3	12%
24—28 moderately deconcentrated	18	41%	92	30%	3	43%	11	32%	11	44%
29—33 moderately concentrated	16	36%	156	52%	1	14%	12	35%	—	28%
34—39 highly con-centrated	8	18%	41	14%	2	29%	4	12%	4	16%

Note: the score for an authority is built up from items such as: Is membership of the policy committee one-party (score 2) or not (score 1)? Is attendance at the policy committee restricted to some chief officers (score 2) or the management team (score 1)? What is the number of corporate groups (6 or 7, score 1; 5 or 6, score 2, etc.)? The scores for these items are added to form a concentration score. A highly deconcentrated authority is one with a score of 18-23; a moderate extent of deconcentration is 24-28; a moderately concentrated score is 29-33; and 34-39 is a highly concentrated score.

Table 3.3 reveals that throughout local government there are noticeable differences in the way that authorities seek to secure policy co-ordination. Some authorities have a highly concentrated style of integration, others do not. In the former authorities the policy committee will be responsible for all strands of resource and policy management either directly or through sub-committees. Authority is concentrated in the hands of a small group of councillors, with service committees expected to route important issues through the policy committee. The policy committee funnels and channels the business of decision-making. Similarly, at officer level there will be a strong chief executive operating through a well-equipped department containing the necessary staff for systems design and policy analysis. In these authorities the involvement of service departments through the procedures of interdepartmental corporate groups is both limited and receives low emphasis. According to Table 3.3 there are 59 authorities of this kind. At the other end of the spectrum are 26 authorities where the style of integration is much less concentrated. Responsibility for all matters of policy and resource co-ordination are not channelled through a single committee. Similarly, policy reports evolve through a network of corporate groups made up of multiple service areas. Interactions are diffuse, and involvement is extensive rather than limited.

Table 3.3 indicates that the overwhelming majority of authorities are between these two extremes. Irrespective of the type of authority there is a clear tendency to be either moderately concentrated or deconcentrated. This is most pronounced in the shire districts where four out of five authorities fall in these midway positions.

There is some evidence, however (drawing upon knowledge of the twenty-seven local authorities), that local authorities are reassessing their integrative styles. Unforeseen events, especially the rapid deterioration of financial circumstances, have occasioned local authorities to reconsider the structures and procedures initiated in 1974. The structures and styles of 1974, based as they were upon the assumptions and circumstances of the 1960s and early 1970s, proved unable to cope with the need for *rapid* decisions in response to central government control over local expenditure. As a result, in some authorities there has been a move towards increasing concentration. This proved to be the case in six of the twenty-seven authorities. In other authorities (twelve of the twenty-seven) the style of integration has remained broadly deconcentrated. Nevertheless, as intimated on p. 47, various changes have begun to emerge at *officer* level. In 1974 a considerable proportion of authorities set up corporate groups for each service. The guiding principle was the programme area, with groups formed for each of the authority's main areas of activity. It was also common to have a member from all, or a majority, of departments on each group. Again, the pressures placed upon the local authority to curb expenditure has begun to expose the difficulties and the strains in operating such an organizational system. It was apparent before the full force of expenditure restraint had been realized that many officers and members were experiencing disillusionment with the system. Corporate groups were seen as cumbersome, time-consuming, and wasteful of resources. The relationships between corporate groups and committees were not clear, neither was that with the management team. Nevertheless, a significant proportion of authorities sustained their commitment to this style of integration but in the force of financial restraints imposed by central government have begun to consider or introduce changes which do not depart from the basic principle of their organizational system. That is, they are retaining a deconcentrated style of integration but introducing modifications so that it can more specifically accommodate the exigencies of financial restraint. Out of the attempt to create comprehensive policies has emerged an identification of the key issues facing the local authority, such as industrial development, the frail, the elderly, the under-fives, rural transport, etc. We have already noted that this has frequently meant the use of clientele as a criterion for differentiation overlaying the service basis of the departmental structure. It also means that the authority is able to retain a deconcentrated style of integration. The problem of slow decision-making is tackled by reducing the scope and composition of the corporate groups. Although fewer areas of the local authority are subject to corporate group analysis the corporate group itself is retained as the principal integrative vehicle at officer level. The integrative style is still a deconcentrated one.

These changes, whether towards greater concentration or to more specific matrix arrangements, are likely to continue over the next few years. Local authorities are exploring different ways of securing appropriate levels of resource and policy co-ordination. In some cases authorities may switch from one style to another: thus, an authority could move from a deconcentrated system based upon the corporate group, to a more concentrated system based upon an executive office. More likely, perhaps, is the confirming of initial arrangements. Authorities towards the concentrated end of the spectrum will move towards greater concentration, whereas deconcentrated authorities will become rationalized while remaining deconcentrated. In other words, an increasing proportion of authorities will move from the moderately concentrated to the highly concentrated category; and an increasing proportion will move from the highly deconcentrated category to the moderately deconcentrated category. Rather less movement will occur from the deconcentrated to the concentrated categories, and vice versa.

Whether these expectations are realized is less important than a more general conclusion, which is that local authorities are likely to continue to exhibit differences in integrative style. The variations in style summarized in Table 3.3 will continue to characterize local government.

SUMMARY

At the beginning of this chapter were laid down two purposes to run through the following analysis. The first and more important of these has been to map organizational similarities and variation throughout local government. That has been attempted using four concepts. Three of these yielded noticeable differences between authorities. Authorities vary in their numbers of service committees and departments (extent of differentiation) and in numbers of co-ordinating committees and departments (extent of integration). Differences were also observed in their styles of integration. Much less variation was found in the kinds of committees and departments being used, with the overwhelming majority of authorities using a combination of service and programme criteria of differentiation. Even so, a number of interesting if minority experiments with area and clientele criteria were discussed. The general conclusion, therefore, is that local authorities exhibit considerable variation in their organizational arrangements. This conclusion will be taken further in the next chapter.

A secondary purpose has been to trace the principal developments of the past fifteen years, and to identify possible changes that might happen in the near future. The discussion of changes since publication of the Report of the Committee on Management has, of necessity, been cursory and restricted to the general features of what have been essentially complex themes. The details of the changes made since 1967 have been outside our compass. Nevertheless, sufficient has been presented to illustrate the changeable character of local authority organizational structures, and to warn the reader to expect further changes in the foreseeable future. We have tentatively identified the broad form that those changes might take.

Given the differences that separate local authority practices, and given their changeable nature, it is imperative that social and political scientists seek to explain why those differences exist, and what prompts them to change. This will form the concern of Chapters 5, 6 and 7. Before doing so, the next chapter picks up our theme that local authorities operate with different kinds of organizational arrangements.

CHAPTER 4

Eight Patterns of Management

INTRODUCTION

Problems of differentiation and integration are of interest not only to students and teachers: they are basic issues of organizational design troubling and exercising the skills and talents of local authority councillors and officers. But these problems tend not to be treated as separate processes. The local authority has to treat organizational design as a problem of combining the processes of differentiation and integration. Analytically these processes may be treated separately, as in Chapter 3; empirically they occur together.

This chapter explores how local authorities have coupled the processes of differentiation and integration. It has already been shown that local authorities vary considerably in their extents of differentiation, integration and concentration.

The important question that must now be asked is whether authorities that are highly differentiated are also those with large numbers of integrative devices and whether these devices constitute a style of high concentration. In other words, do authorities with many service committees and departments also have many integrative committees and departments; or, is the extent of differentiation unrelated to the extent of integration? These and similar questions are the concern of this chapter.

There are eight possible organizational patterns, as indicated in Table 4.1. That figure combines three of the four structural issues discussed in Chapters 2 and 3: the fourth, criteria of differentiation, is omitted from the following analysis because of the lack of variation previously established.

Pattern A is a combination of low differentiation, high integration

67

TABLE 4.1   *Eight Patterns of Organization*

	Integration	Differentiation	
		Extent	
Extent	Style	Low	High
High	Concentrated	Pattern A	Pattern E
High	Deconcentrated	Pattern B	Pattern F
Low	Concentrated	Pattern C	Pattern G
Low	Deconcentrated	Pattern D	Pattern H

and high concentration. An authority with such a pattern has comparatively few service committees, sub-committees and departments, but many integrative structures such as a policy and resource committee, and sub-committees, a network of interdepartmental corporate groups, and several specialist functional units. Furthermore, the routing of issues is concentrated through the management team and the policy committee. Participation is limited. Pattern D, in contrast, is a combination of low differentiation with little and deconcentrated structural integration. These authorities have few service committees and departments, and few arrangements for their co-ordination. The arrangements for co-ordination which do exist emphasize a deconcentrated style, with wide participation and a limited role for the policy committee. The other patterns can be similarly described.

In order to find out how many authorities operate with each of the eight patterns some means is required for identifying a high or low score on the three organizational variables. How do we decide that an authority's structural arrangements constitute high as opposed to low extents of differentiation/integration/concentration?

The method pursued here has been to rank authorities in terms of each other. An authority is classified as being highly differentiated if other authorities on average tend to have fewer committees and departments. Similarly, a highly integrated authority is one with more than the average number of integrative committees and departments.

Table 4.2 indicates the number of authorities operating with each of the organizational patterns, ranking authorities in terms of the average scores for all authorities. For example, there are 55 authorities with pattern A, 83 with pattern D, and so forth. The table is, however, misleading in an important respect. For reasons that need not detain us unduly here interesting variations, especially among the shire districts, are obscured. The large proportion of shire districts (302 of 412) tend to weight the averages around which authorities are classified in Table 4.3. The shire districts, because of their noticeably different and much more limited range of functions are almost always found with 'below average' scores. To overcome this unnecessary distortion Table 4.3 treats the shire districts as a separate sample, with the scores of all other authorities summarized in Table 4.4. Table 4.3 demonstrates the frequency of each organizational pattern based upon the average scores for shire districts; Table 4.4 uses the average scores of all other authorities. These tables simply reinforce the conclusions of Chapter 3 — that there are significant differences between authorities.

Authorities vary in their *combination* of responses to critical structural issues. In other words there are two sorts of variation. First, authorities vary in terms of (for example) their numbers of service committees and departments. That is, differences exist in the extent of differentiation. Secondly, authorities with the *same* extent of differentiation may well *differ* along a second dimension,

TABLE 4.2   *Eight Patterns of Organization: Number of Authorities in Each Category*

Integration		Differentiation	
Extent	Style	Low	High
High	Concentration	(A) 55	(E) 48
High	Deconcentration	(B) 41	(F) 60
Low	Concentration	(C) 79	(G) 27
Low	Deconcentration	(D) 83	(H) 19

TABLE 4.3   *Eight Patterns of Organization: Shire Districts*

Integration		Differentiation			
Extent	Style	Low		High	
High	Concentration	(A)	45	(E)	35
High	Deconcentration	(B)	35	(F)	40
Low	Concentration	(C)	46	(G)	37
Low	Deconcentration	(D)	45	(H)	19

TABLE 4.4   *Eight Patterns of Organization: Non-Shire Districts*

Integration		Differentiation			
Extent	Style	Low		High	
High	Concentration	(A)	15	(E)	13
High	Deconcentration	(B)	18	(F)	12
Low	Concentration	(C)	11	(G)	15
Low	Deconcentration	(D)	16	(H)	10

namely in their extent and style of integration. Thus, some of the authorities with large numbers of service committees and departments have few co-ordinating arrangements (low integration) whereas others have many. Put this way the structural variation throughout local government is seen to be both extensive and complex. In one sense Tables 4.3 and 4.4 suffice for the immediate task of this chapter which is to demonstrate how far local authorities vary in their combined responses to several structural issues. But those tables can be used to go a step further.

A further description of the characteristics of each organizational pattern will sharpen the differences between them. We shall also consider a number of operational difficulties that seem to be associated with certain patterns. In doing so attention will be concentrated upon two basic forms of organization:

(1) authorities with high integration and low differentiation (patterns A and B)
(2) authorities with low integration and high differentiation (patterns G and H)

These four patterns represent ends of a continuum. At one extreme is an authority which places considerable emphasis upon the pursuit of integration. It does so by creating structural machinery for the express purpose of integrating the activities and decisions of other structural units, and by reducing as far as possible the numbers of those 'other' structural units. The thrust of this basic organizational form is the attainment of co-ordination. At the other extreme is a form of organization which pursues the advantages of specialization. In these organizations there is little attempt to create structural machinery for the purposes of co-ordination. The degree of co-ordination perceived to be necessary is less than that perceived in patterns A and B and the advantages of co-ordination are seen to be outweighed by the disadvantages of limiting the process of differentiation. In these organizations the advantage of specialization and the heightened level of professional commitment often associated with it are seen to outweigh the possible costs of the duplication of, and overlap and inconsistencies in, policies prepared by relatively independent committees and departments.

Between these two positions are various intermediary states, including patterns C—F. Our concern, however, will be primarily with the two extreme forms: that is, with patterns A and B on the one hand, and G and H on the other. The following sections describe the characteristics of these patterns in order to explore the kinds of procedural difficulties and dilemmas that are, or might be, associated with such characteristics. The reader is reminded that the description of structural characteristics is based upon the sample of 412 authorities, whereas the interpretive exploration will use material from the sample of twenty-seven authorities which has been studied in more detail.

PATTERN A

There are forty-five shire districts and fifteen other local authorities with the structures of pattern A. This latter group includes six shire and one metropolitan county, seven metropolitan districts and one London borough.

The committee structures of these authorities have two distinctive features. First, there are several committees or sub-committees intended to ensure that the processes of policymaking and resource allocation are pursued in integrated fashion. Secondly, the committee structures are concentrated. Thus, most of the central co-ordinating functions are the responsibility of a single policy and resources committee, or of *sub*-committees reporting directly to it. For example, four out of every five non-shire authorities have a personnel sub-committee, and a land sub-committee. A further two out of every three authorities have a finance sub-committee. In the shire districts the proportions are not dissimilar. Four out of five of them have a personnel sub-committee, and almost two thirds have a land sub-committee, and a performance review sub-committee. Finance sub-committees are found in slightly above one-half of these authorities. These statistics emphasize the point that under pattern A it is unusual for responsibility for the resource functions to be given full committee status: they are seen as part of the wider responsibilities of the policy committee. The processes of resource allocation (land, personnel and finance) are organizationally combined at the point at which central policy co-ordination is exercised.

The emphasis upon concentrated co-ordination of decision making is reinforced by the general practice, found in approximately four out of every five shire districts and two out of every three non-shire authorities, of having all chief officers of the management team in attendance at the policy committee. This contrasts sharply with more traditional arrangements in which the central committee would be serviced by the clerk and the treasurer with other officers invited to attend as necessary. By having all chief officers in attendance at the policy committee there is a clear emphasis placed upon their responsibility to that committee, in a way that reduces the status of, although does not remove, the link between the service chief officer and the service committee chairman. This difference will be elaborated later, in discussing patterns G and H. However, there are a number of other issues appropriately raised at this juncture to do with the concentration of relationships through the policy committee.

The reporting relationships of officers to members (that is, whether those relationships should involve collective reports to the policy committee or individual reports to a service committee chairman) is the first of at least four issues concerning interactions between officers and members. One of these, to do with whether the management team should adopt a stance of collective responsibility, will be discussed in the next section as it affects both patterns A and B. The remaining issues, however, are more conveniently raised here. One of these is to do with their *accountability*. For purposes of analysis a distinction may be drawn between two alternative conceptions as to how officers should be accountable to members. These may be described as the 'civil service model' and the 'local government model'. The former model sees the administration serving the majority party, not the council as a whole. This, of course, is the model applied in central government. The latter model treats members as equal, and gives them equal access to both information and advice. It rejects the notion of excluding a proportion of the council from important stages within the processes of policy-making and budgeting. It does not recognize the majority party as possessing special power and status. The distinction between these models is interestingly illustrated by the control of committee agendas. Thus, authorities operating the civil service model allow senior members of the majority party to determine whether, and when, an item will appear on the committee agenda. The local government model would have the agenda determined by the press of business, as interpreted by the chief officer concerned. The committee chairman might well be briefed about business coming before a committee, and he may discuss with the chief officer how the various items of business can be handled at the committee meeting, but he would not be allowed either to remove items from the agenda, or to shape the chief officer's reports.

There has always been variation throughout local government on the use of these models. Some authorities have approximated rather more towards the civil service model than other authorities. These authorities recognize explicitly the existence of political parties and in a sense, have adopted an officer—member relationship consistent with that recognition. In general, however, our impression is that in the pre-Reorganization era local authorities tended more towards the local government model of accountability than to the civil service model. The years following Reorganization have seen an increasing politicization (Rhodes, 1975; Jennings, 1975, 1977) of many local authorities, and, partly as a consequence, there has been a movement amongst certain authorities towards the civil service model. In these authorities the majority parties have assumed exclusive responsibility for key decision areas and asserted control over sources of information and advice. In these authorities the officers clearly see themselves as serving the majority party.

The distinction between these two models of accountability can be overstated. No local authority could operate in the same way as the civil service, in that the administration is not insulated from members of minority parties. Nor would local authorities necessarily wish to operate entirely along the lines of the civil service. On the contrary, there are frequent interactions between officers and councillors of all political parties, interactions often seen as useful by both minority party members and the chief officer and his staff. Nevertheless, our researches (Hinings *et al.*, 1980) have identified changes in the orientations of officers in their dealings with members. There is a significant number of authorities in which chief officers are finding it convenient to reassess how they should relate to members. These officers are openly wondering whether they should treat members as equals (and effectively ignore the existence of political parties) or whether they should recognize responsibility to the majority party.*

This is an issue which is affecting authorities other than those with pattern A structures. It is found, to a greater or lesser extent, in all organizational patterns. But it does seem particularly pertinent to pattern A authorities in that the committee structure of these authorities fits the model of a council run along cabinet lines. That is, there is a concentrated committee structure which places the lines of influence and information in the hands of a small group of senior members who are usually the leaders of the majority party. We are hypothesizing, in other words, that pattern A authorities may well be those more likely to operate a civil service model of accountability.

---

*This is developed further in Hinings *et al.* (1980), who find that the dominant model in the post-Reorganization era is the civil service model, and that this model has become *increasingly* operated.

The third issue concerning how officers relate to members is to do with the composition of the policy committee and the place of the party caucus. Prior to Reorganization there was a clear and growing tendency for local authorities to make the central policy committee a single party committee (Greenwood *et al.,* 1972). And, in that members of the policy committee would usually be the major service committee chairmen, this tendency can be seen as a step in the direction of a cabinet form of local organization. Indeed, in the years preceding Reorganization Greenwood *et al.* were prompted to remark that:

> The advantages of the one-party policy committee — it links the policy committee with the procedures of political co-ordination and allows officers of the authority to properly advise the party leadership — make it an attractive proposition. It is possible that the one-party policy committee will become the main form of policy committee in the future and contribute towards the introduction of cabinet government at the local level. [1972, p. 165]

The Report of the Bains Working Group argued against this trend. The view expressed was that local democracy would be better served by the inclusion of councillors from the minority parties as members of the policy committee. Their reasoning is not our concern here, but it is important to note that the result of the Working Group's recommendations was an interruption in the growth of one-party policy committees. The trend is unlikely to be halted altogether. It is probable that in the next few years additional local authorities will recognize that party groups are taking direct responsibility for important council decisions, and will wish to recognize this fact by composing the central policy committee of representatives from one party. In this way the party would be able to formally control the machinery of decision making, both with the open advice of officers and without paying lip-service to the myth that control is exercised in conjunction with minority parties. It is also our view that one-party policy committees will become the dominant practice of authorities within pattern A structures. A concentrated committee structure, coupled with a discernible trend towards a civil service model of officer accountability, seems to be consistent with a one-party policy committee. The single-party policy committee, in other words, is an organizational complement to other structural characteristics of pattern A.

Co-ordination at officer level in pattern A authorities is orchestrated by the chief executive who will almost always have a department. Not for these chief executives the idea that they should operate without immediate departmental support. Admittedly, the scale of the department varies from authority to authority but there will be a department, and it will include *several* functions, such as corporate and policy analysis, research and intelligence, personnel management, project co-ordination, and, although less often, responsibility for management services (see Table 4.5). The chief executive will tend not to have responsibility for the more traditional functions of committee administration and legal services, but it is not uncommon for his department to have a close involvement in the servicing of the policy committee. This is especially likely to be the case in the non-shire districts.

These observations clearly demonstrate that within pattern A authorities the chief executive has assumed a direct responsibility for some of the organizational instruments of policy co-ordination. They also indicate that the instruments of *financial* management are rarely attached directly to the chief executive, despite a number of exceptions. Generally speaking the concept of the executive office set out in the Paterson Report is not a characteristic of pattern A authorities.

It is unclear whether the existing separation of responsibility for finance from the policy responsibilities of the chief executive will remain a permanent feature of English local government. Research into the sample of 27 local authorities makes it increasingly evident that over the past few years chief executives have been building 'special relationships' with either the director of finance and/or the finance officer with particular responsibility for financial planning. The role of the chief executive has become much more closely associated with some of the financial functions traditionally left in the hands of the director of finance. That is, there is an increasing recognition of the need for the chief executive to develop a direct organizational capacity that will enable him to influence and shape the processes both of policy formulation and of resource allocation. In this respect some authorities are moving further from the ideas of Bains towards those of Paterson. It is an intriguing question whether chief executives will in the future find it necessary, or convenient, to develop direct responsibility for certain functions hitherto located within the finance department. We would expect

TABLE 4.5 *Number and Type of Functions in the Chief Executive's Department by Organizational Pattern*

	Non-Shire Districts								Shire Districts							
	A	B	C	D	E	F	G	H	A	B	C	D	E	F	G	H
No. of functions (average)	6	3	5	2	5	2	7	5	5	3	6	4	5	4	6	4
Type of function[a]																
Corporate planning	12	8	7	5	11	6	12	2	36	16	41	16	26	26	29	9
Research and intelligence	10	1	5	4	9	2	5	2	21	4	23	9	14	7	17	3
Personnel	9	3	6	1	8	2	11	7	35	17	36	21	25	20	32	9
Public relations	11	4	8	2	9	1	14	5	39	18	42	19	26	20	31	12
Legal services	3	1	3	1	4	0	10	5	13	4	21	6	12	6	20	6
Management services	6	2	7	1	7	1	11	5	32	11	29	10	20	17	27	5
Committee administration	3	5	5	1	6	0	11	4	14	4	26	9	12	10	25	5
No. of authorities	15	18	11	16	13	12	15	10	45	35	46	45	35	40	37	19

[a] This list is not exhaustive.

these developments, if they do occur, to be more likely within authorities currently operating under pattern A.

The position at the moment, however, is this: in pattern A authorities the chief executive has a department containing several non-financial functions that enable him to influence the processes of policy formulation and implementation. Responsibility for finance is with the director of finance with whom the chief executive will have a close relationship.

Not all the necessary interdepartmental co-ordination could be arranged or secured through a central department. In addition the chief executive of a pattern A authority will be supported by a management team and a network of up to six interdepartmental corporate groups. In the shire districts the number of corporate groups rarely goes above three (13 per cent have more); in the other authorities it is common to have between four and six groups. These figures are not dissimilar to those found in pattern B authorities.

Pattern A differs markedly from pattern B, however, in the composition of the management team and of the corporate groups. Interdepartmental corporate groups under pattern A will be composed of 'relevant' rather than all departments. Pattern A authorities are selective and restrictive in membership whereas pattern B authorities tend *at the moment* to be all-inclusive. This selective arrangement is found in all authorities of pattern A. The composition of the management team varies by type of authority. Shire districts within pattern A include all chief officers. Other authorities, by contrast, are much more likely to exclude some chief officers. Nearly two-thirds of these authorities exclude a number of service chief officers.

The above arrangements contribute to the following pattern. Pattern A authorities are characterized by a committee structure in which co-ordinative arrangements centre upon a single policy committee to which all chief officers report and are accountable. There will be a chief executive operating with a comparatively large department supported by both a management team and a number of corporate groups of limited memberships. The whole thrust of this organizational pattern is for a concentration of information and decision through these integrative structures, with responsibility centrally located rather than diffused throughout the organization. Over time these authorities might develop other characteristics such as (a) a closer relationship between the role of the chief executive and responsibility for financial forecasting and (b) the creation of a one-party policy committee. It is likely that these authorities will operate the civil service model of account-ability, and will experience tensions associated with the collective responsibility of management team members.

PATTERN B

Thirty-five shire districts, three metropolitan counties, eight shire counties, one metropolitan district and six London boroughs have structures of pattern B. In many respects the committee structures of these authorities are similar to those of pattern A. They share the same emphasis upon the pursuit of policy coordination and resource allocation, and have structures explicitly set up for this purpose. The striking discord between patterns A and B is that under the latter responsibility for such matters as the co-ordination of finance, of personnel, of land, and of performance review are given committee rather than sub-committee status. Instead of routing all matters of policy and resource co-ordination through a single point, namely the policy and resources committee, there are often several full co-ordinating committees each with its own links with service committees and the council. The structure of the authority is more diffuse and less concentrated than under pattern A.

In one respect the committee system of pattern B is *not* deconcentrated. In Chapter 3 it was suggested that a fully deconcentrated system would restrict the attendance of chief officers at the policy committee. Such a system would place less emphasis upon the responsibility of chief officers to the central policy committee, preferring instead to retain the relationship between the service chief officer and 'his' committee chairman. This is not the case in pattern B. A considerable majority of pattern B authorities expect all chief officers to attend the policy committee. This indicates a desire to overcome one of the strongest traditional obstacles to the pursuit of policy co-ordination, that is, the chief officer/chairman relationship. Even those authorities with a basically deconcentrated form of organization have felt it necessary to put some emphasis both upon the role of the policy committee, and upon the responsibility of all chief officers to it.

Hence, the attendance of all chief officers at meetings of the policy committee.

Co-ordination of the officer structure is more consistently deconcentrated. Pattern B authorities have a chief executive, usually with a *small* department. In the shire districts the functions more commonly found under the chief executive are personnel, public relations and corporate planning. Much less common is the chief executive with direct responsibility for committee administration and legal services (4 authorities out of 35). Chief executives in the non-shire authorities often have responsibility only for corporate planning. Only one of them has responsibility for legal services.

This pattern of responsibilities indicates two important points. First, the chief executive has concentrated upon those functions to do with policy co-ordination. There is a clear attempt to focus attention on matters other than traditional functions such as committee administration and legal services. Similarly, there has been little attempt to assume direct responsibility for the management of finance. In this respect pattern B differs little from pattern A. Secondly, however (and this *is* different from pattern A), the chief executive has limited the scale of his department in order to work through a management team containing *all* departmental chief officers assisted by a network of interdepartmental corporate groups. In these authorities much less attention is placed upon the idea of a strong central departmental capacity and rather more upon the role of the management team and corporate groups. There is emphasis upon securing the co-operation and commitment of service departments by involving them directly in the co-ordination of activities. This is not to suggest, however, that all departments will be represented on all corporate groups. As indicated earlier, pressures of time often prevent such a pattern of working. Nevertheless, the basic officer structure is of a deconcentrated form.

There are a number of operational issues associated with this organizational pattern. Three issues in particular will be discussed: the confusion of responsibility and relationships, the heavy consumption of time, and the extent to which officers should adopt a collective responsibility for the preparation of advice for members.

The inherent difficulty of using interdepartmental corporate groups (including the management team of chief officers) is that they cut across traditional and well-understood lines of accountability.

The traditional sequence of accountability for the preparation of advice on policy has been from the chief officer, as head of the appropriate service department, to the service committee and thence to the full council. That arrangement was, and is, well understood. The introduction of corporate groups, however, cuts across that arrangement. For example, a director of social services may find that one of his staff is a member of a corporate group discussing services for the elderly. How should the director relate either to his member of staff, and/or to the corporate group? Does he allow the member of staff sufficient discretion to commit the department to various courses of action?

Similarly, what are the relationships between the corporate group, the chief officer and the management team? Does the corporate group report directly to the management team? Or should the affected chief officer be allowed to receive and consider (and rewrite?) reports in advance of other chief officers? Which chief officer would take the report to committee? And to *which* committee(s): policy or service? It is outside our brief to provide answers to these and similar questions. Our purpose is to expose the confused reporting relationships and patterns of procedural accountability, that are associated with the use of corporate groups. In that pattern B authorities emphasize corporate groups, such authorities are likely to experience these difficulties in acute form.

The difficulties of operating a system of corporate groups are compounded by the heavy consumption of time which they involve at a time when local authorities are squeezing, rather than expanding, their manpower resources. It is apparent from the study of 27 local authorities that many officers and members are becoming disillusioned with the fuller forms of pattern B structures set up in 1974. Then, the dominant practice was to set up a corporate group for each service. Thus, there might be a housing group, a leisure group, a social services group, an education group and so on, depending upon the type of local authority. It was also likely that a member of all, or at least a majority of, departments would be involved. In practice this meant the staffing of corporate groups with second, third and fourth-tier officers. The tasks of these groups were to produce policy programmes for the authority, feeding them through the management team to the relevant committee. Experience with these arrangements proved them to be rather cumbersome, time-consuming and time-wasting. Some of these difficulties were outlined in an earlier chapter. As a result the structures and processes of pattern B authorities are being revised. Out of the attempt to create comprehensive policies has come an identification of the 'key issues' facing the local authority, issues such as industrial development, the elderly, rural transport, and so on. Organizationally the response has been rationalization of the corporate group structure. The problems of slow decision-making are overcome by reducing both the scope and the size of corporate groups. Instead of a concern with the totality of issues facing a particular programme area, the groups concentrate on key issues. Despite these changes, however, pattern B authorities are still frequently seen as wasteful of officers' time, and slow in the process of decision-making. Whether pattern B can overcome these difficulties remains to be seen.

These changes in the network of corporate groups lead to the third issue affecting pattern B authorities. It is the issue noted above as relevant to pattern A authorities, but which was held over for discussion here. One of the difficulties of local authorities in the post-Reorganization era has been the fact that members are suspicious both of the role of the management team, and of the chief executive officer. There is a widespread concern that the management team under the leadership of the chief executive is subverting the role of the member. Members believe that officers are taking decisions which they themselves should be taking. This is not, of course, a novel concern: it was present in the findings of the Maud Committee on Management in 1967. But the sheer visibility of the management team, and of the chief executive, since Reorganization, has exacerbated these suspicions. Ironically, these suspicions are expressed even where the management team exercises very little influence. One of the frequent complaints expressed by chief officers (of all organizational patterns) is the *inadequacy* of the management team, especially its tendency to discuss trivia, rather than matter of significance.

Not all management teams discuss trivia. Some have arrangements ensuring that important issues are debated and analysed before reports are submitted to members. An interesting question facing all management teams, however, concerns the style of the report that goes forward; in particular, how far the management team should exercise *collective* responsibility when meeting members. This issue is emerging to a greater or lesser extent in all authorities irrespective of their organizational pattern, but it may well become of particular concern to patterns A and B. Consider the following alternative possibilities. At one extreme a management team can discuss matters and, having arrived at a collective conclusion, insist that chief officers *actively support* that conclusion when the item is discussed in committees, thus ignoring reservations which may have been expressed during the deliberations of the management team. There will be a very clear understanding that chief officers do not speak against the team's report and its recommendations at committee. Similarly, the chief executive will frown upon the practice of chief officers 'briefing' the committee chairmen against the report. At the other extreme is the practice where no management team reports are presented, with individual chief officers reporting through the management team to committee, but where the chief officer is not obliged to alter his report in the light of any discussions he may have had with his colleagues either individually or in the management team. Moreover, chief officers may, and will, express their open disagreement with that report, or passages and recommendations within it, at member level.

Most authorities lie somewhere along a continuum between these two positions. The latter position is the more traditional in local government. The former is the one creating difficulties. If co-ordinated working is to be achieved the management team has to produce reports which chief officers are prepared to support. On the other hand, to do so may confirm the suspicions of members that officers are assuming too great an influence and exercising the authority which is properly their's as elected representatives. Unless members receive overt evidence of disagreement between chief officers, they tend to assume that chief officers are concealing that disagreement. As a result there are instances of party leaders attending and chairing the management team, changing the composition of the team, and even disbanding the team. The product of suspicion has often been structural surgery.

These tensions and suspicions are not confined to patterns A and B. They occur in authorities with other structural arrangements. However, we would *expect* them to occur rather more frequently under patterns A and B because it is these authorities that have the greatest number of active management teams and it is these authorities that have a tendency to develop collective responsibility. The pursuit of co-ordinated advice is not far removed from the presentation of limited options backed up by the collective view of a management team. We might reasonably expect these practices to foster a degree of member—officer suspicion, and a measure of tension. One of the crucial difficulties within patterns A and B is likely to be the satisfactory management (but not necessarily the removal) of that tension.

PATTERNS G AND H

Patterns G and H represent the opposite end of a continuum from patterns A and B. Much less emphasis is placed upon the value of structural co-ordination and rather more upon the advantages of differentiation. In this section we shall discuss patterns G and H together in order to highlight their differences from patterns A and B. In doing so, the discussion will point to differences between patterns G and H, but these are minimal, rather than extensive. It is this lack of marked differences between G and H that warrants them receiving concurrent, rather than separate discussion.

There are thirty-seven shire districts with pattern G structures and a further nineteen with pattern H. In addition, there are eight shire counties, two metropolitan districts and five London boroughs with pattern G, and four shire counties, three metropolitan districts and three London boroughs with pattern H.

The integrative arrangements found under pattern G are similar to those recommended by the Bains Working Group. At committee level there is usually a policy and resources committee with three or four sub-committees for the management of finance, personnel, land and performance review. The policy committee normally includes representatives from all the political parties represented on the council. At officer level there is a chief executive officer at the head of a management team, which in turn is assisted by a small number of interdepartmental corporate groups. Neither the management team nor the corporate groups necessarily include all chief officers or their representatives. All these structural features are found within the Bains Working Group Report, or are closely linked with the logic of that report.

Pattern G authorities deviate from the Bains Report on the question of a chief executive's department. Almost all authorities within pattern G have such a department. This is not, of course, dissimilar from some of the authorities found in other organizational patterns but pattern G is remarkable for the size of that department. The department is *larger* than in most other authorities, containing an average of seven functions in the non-shire districts and six in the shire districts. The particular functions that will be found within it are indicated in Table 4.5. It is noticeable that the list of functions includes those traditional responsibilities of the Clerk's department which are now often separated from the chief executive within a department of administration. Not surprisingly, separate departments of administration are rarely found under pattern G.

The difference between patterns G and H is that under the latter system responsibility for co-ordination of finance, personnel, and land will be given full committee status. There is no attempt to follow the idea set out within the Bains Report that these functions should be routed through a central policy and resources committee. These authorities do follow Bains in that the policy committee usually consists of representatives from all political parties. In other words, the integrative system of pattern H is essentially deconcentrated. At officer level there is a chief executive with a department (see Table 4.5) supported by a management team composed of at least a majority and more usually all chief officers. Those chief officers attend the policy committee. Corporate groups exist but are few in number. In other words, the principal differences between authorities exhibiting patterns G and H are that the latter have a less concentrated committee structure, a smaller chief executive's department, and a management team made up of a larger proportion of chief officers.

Both patterns G and H reflect the grafting onto traditional structures of the bare minimum number of integrative structures consistent with the recommendations set out in the Bains Report. These authorities have been influenced, but only to a limited extent, by the tidal wash of ideas about corporate planning which swept through local government in the later 1960s and early 1970s. They have retitled the Clerk as chief executive and added to the functions within his department. They have retitled the finance committee and given it responsibilities more akin to the management of policy. These changes are consistent with the salient notions and structural prescriptions of the movement for corporate planning. They represent the grafting onto traditional arrangements of the minimum set of ideas to do with policy co-ordination. The changes introduced involve little radical alteration to existing arrangements.

Patterns G and H in other words place much less emphasis upon the design of structural machinery for purposes of co-ordination than patterns A and B. Inevitably, therefore, the operational issues in these authorities are of a different form from those of patterns A and B. New structures inevitably produce tensions and difficulties as the relationships between different parts of the local authority are evolved and negotiated, and in patterns G and H the prevalent issues centre around the process of *rejecting* the new structures: that is, under G and H the operational issues illustrate that the structural grafting has failed. This may be illustrated with reference firstly to the role of the policy committee, and secondly to that of the management team.

The problem confronting the policy committee is often its relationship with the finance committee or sub-committee. The Bains Report wanted to divorce responsibility for finance from that for policy in order to avoid matters of policy becoming drowned in the details of resource allocation. If, however, there is no extensive attempt at central policy co-ordination (as is the tendency in patterns G and H) then the question becomes, what should be the role of the policy committee? This has proved to be a rather less intractable problem under pattern G, in that the policy committee has simply absorbed responsibility for resource allocation and either treats the finance sub-committee as a largely redundant body, or uses it for detailed matters of financial management. A pattern H authority, however, finds such an arrangement more difficult to conceive because full committees are less willing to give up their responsibilities. Attempts by the policy committee to act as the major financial committee, and as little more than that, lead to resentment on the part of the finance committee and to confused and possibly bitter relationships. In these authorities the relationship between the policy committee and the finance committee is both unclear and, sometimes, fractious.

The issue confronting the position of the chief executive is what should be done with those parts of the officer structure that do not correspond with the basically traditional management system within which they are set. For example, what should be the role of the management team? Given that the routing of information is primarily from chief officer to committee, and given that there is little expectation by members and officers that officers will attempt extensive co-ordination of departmental affairs, there is little for the management team to do. There are, of course, various matters which must be the responsibility of the management team, such as consideration of revenue estimates and the capital programme. But these matters are not sufficient to maintain a regular and frequent cycle of meetings. Hence, it is these authorities where one finds a growing incidence of complaints that the management team and the sub-structure of corporate groups are a waste of time because they are concerned with trivia. Unlike patterns A and B, where the criticisms are of excessive interference and centralization, under patterns G and H the complaints are about futility and irrelevance.

The primary organizational issues under patterns G and H, therefore, are concerned with making some use of the structural devices intended for a rather different form of management from that actually existing within the local authority. This means that what these structures do, and the way they relate to other parts of the local authority, are likely to be very different from what happens within patterns A and B. The terms used may be the same — policy committee, management team — but what they *do* differs markedly under the different organizational patterns. It is also, of course, in these authorities (that is, those with patterns G and H) that there is often pressure to let the newer structures wither away. The corporate group structure in particular becomes defunct, and the management team a comparatively insignificant body. The chief executive remains, but acts as a traditional clerk, and the policy committee seeks to interpret its role as the co-ordinator of resource allocation and financial control. If these developments do take place then patterns G and H will become even further divorced from the ideas and practices of patterns A and B.

PATTERNS C, D, E AND F

The patterns discussed so far are towards opposite ends of a continuum. Patterns C, D, E and F represent positions between those ends. A total of 166 of the shire districts fall in these categories and 52 non-shire districts. A more detailed breakdown of the latter figure is given in Table 4.6.

TABLE 4.6   *Types of Authority and Patterns of Organization*

Type of Authority	Pattern			
	C	D	E	F
Shire Counties	3	4	7	4
Metropolitan Districts	3	7	4	7
Metropolitan Counties	1	1	1	0
London Boroughs	4	4	1	1
Total	11	16	13	12

Each of these patterns is a combination of features already discussed in some detail in previous sections. Patterns C and D, for example, have structures that resemble the authorities with patterns A and B except that much less organizational emphasis is placed upon the pursuit of integration. There are fewer co-ordinating committees and sub-committees, and a more moderate use of interdepartmental corporate groups. Nevertheless, in basic outline patterns C and D approximate towards patterns A and B. What this means in terms of operational difficulties and problems is unclear and there is insufficient data at hand to put forward propositions concerning the workings of patterns C and D. What would be interesting for future research would be to examine whether these patterns, which seem to be half-steps towards A and B, move towards a fuller expression of their basic form. Are they, in effect, embryonic forms of patterns A and B? And, what circumstances will push them towards a clearer adoption of those patterns?

Similar reservations and suggestions can be made for patterns E and F. These authorities have characteristics in common both with patterns G and H (high rates of differentiation) and with patterns A and B (high extents of integration). In one sense, therefore, patterns E and F are rather more balanced than any of the other patterns in that these authorities have attempted to secure the advantages of both differentiation and of integration. According to Lawrence and Lorsch (1967) it is these authorities that should attain higher measures of performance, although it is debatable whether such an easy conclusion is applicable to the kinds of organizations within our sample.

There may well be, however, particular difficulties associated with patterns E and F. High differentiation coupled with high integration means that the authority has a considerable number of service committees and sub-committees each supported by a professional department. These structures correspond to traditional policy arrangements and are likely to maintain the same pattern of accountability and responsibility as described by the Committee on Management (1967). Service departments will report to 'their' service committees and will regard themselves as answerable and accountable to those committees. Similarly, the committee will see itself as primarily concerned with the service, and expect the department to act through the committee. That is, having set up committees and departments responsible for a discrete set of functions it is unreasonable to suppose that they will not maintain the traditional chief officer/committee chairman bond. However, these authorities have a countervailing set of structures intended to nullify the worse excesses of traditional arrangements. There will be a network of central co-ordinating committees and sub-committees, a chief executive, probably with a department, supported by a management team, various specialist functional units, and a series of corporate groups. There will, of course, be differences between patterns E and F in much the same way as the style of integration within pattern A differed from that of pattern B. But they share the important characteristic of having *many* integrative structures. These structures seek to introduce new patterns of interaction and accountability. The chief executive will attempt to persuade or instruct service chief officers to take important matters of policy to the management team. He will seek to subject matters of importance to analysis by corporate groups or by experts within his own department. Similarly, an active policy committee will seek to comment upon and ensure consistency between the policies agreed within the service committee advised by the service departments. The policy committee will wish to constrain the policies of different service areas in order to blend them into an integrated whole. In doing all of this the integrative structures will run against the more traditional ways of doing things, ways still embodied in the service committee/service department structures.

All authorities with more than the minimum number of integrative structures face the problem of meshing the newer approaches with the old. Patterns A and B have arguably the greater chance of successfully developing the newer approaches to policy co-ordination. These authorities have consistently designed the local authority structure with this purpose in mind. The traditional lines of accountability have been scaled down in importance in favour of relationships consolidating the role and status of the newer integrative structures. Patterns E and F, in contrast, have not reduced the importance of traditional lines of accountability. These authorities have placed both traditional and corporate approaches side by side. Inevitably, there will be stresses and conflicts as the various participants attempt to sustain their preferred course of action. For this reason it is these authorities (patterns E and F) that may face the greater degree of instability. Throughout this book our attention is upon the relationship between environmental and organizational circumstances, and structural form. The role of values and political interest as determinants of organizational change has been deliberately ignored. These forces *are* extremely important and will be considered further in the concluding chapter. But it is worth making brief reference here to the possibility that local authorities which have, deliberately or otherwise, pursued the advantages of both policy co-ordination (through the creation of integrative structures) and of differentiation (large numbers of service committees and departments) may be those that experience the greatest struggles between those officers and members committed to the traditional practices, and those committed to the development of the corporate approach.

SUMMARY

In this chapter local authorities have been arranged into eight organizational patterns in order to demonstrate the variation that exists throughout local government. Each organizational pattern has been described, and some attempts have been made to identify the difficulties that may be associated with them. Much of the discussion has drawn upon the material collected from the sample of twenty-seven local authorities. The numbers of authorities operating with each of the eight organizational patterns were calculated from the questionnaire to all local authorities, but the propositions and expectations concerning the operational difficulties of those patterns were taken from the sample of twenty-seven. It is important that the reader appreciate that much of the discussion in this chapter is rather more tentative than that of Chapter 3.

What can be stated with certainty, however, is that the organizational practices of local authorities differ, and in some ways differ considerably. In Chapter 3 the differences were summarized in terms of four structural ideas, each taken separately. In this chapter three of the issues were combined to show the relative incidence of alternative organizational patterns. Thus, we have concluded the initial task of this book which has been to describe the extent and principal differences between local authority structural practices. Remaining chapters turn to the second task, and seek to *explain* these differences. The framework of ideas and concepts necessary for this purpose is set out in the following chapter.

CHAPTER 5

Why Do Local Authorities Differ?
Why Do They Change?

INTRODUCTION

On 6 July 1976 the Conservative-led Birmingham City Council approved a resolution which called for the replacement of the system of corporate management introduced three years earlier. Supporting the resolution, the leader of the Conservative Party, Councillor Neville B. A. Bosworth, made the following criticisms of the corporate system:

> I have come to the conclusion that the erosion of the power of committees to determine their own policy and control the adminis-tration of their own department has gone too far. I want committees to get on with the basic local government job delegated to them without too much interference and I want Chief Officers to carry out their department's functions without the multiplicity of groups, sub-groups, multi-disciplinary teams and working parties, which tend to work independently of Chief Officers and departments. If for example, one examines the proposals for the Programme Area Groups, one sees up to eleven senior officers with the function of considering subject areas loosely defined as economic, social and physical. The chairmanship was to have rotated — one might have a third tier officer in the Amenities and Recreation Department reporting to the Chairman of the Education Committee on education matters. No less than 31 officers at first, second or third tier level would be spending one morning or an afternoon a fortnight at these meetings — one-ninth of their working time on this alone.
>
> I do not consider that the attempt to administer the City as a single entity with all the staff working within a so-called 'corporate framework' has met with much success. Indeed, in my view the system was never fully understood even by some of those who were charged with operating it and it appears to me that the Principal Chief Officers' Management Team failed to have any significant

92

impact on the management of the authority. We had a lot of theory and complex systems were introduced which proved unworkable.

There comes to mind some of the results:

(a) Though the question of area administration and mini town halls has been discussed by the Principal Chief Officers' Management Team for a couple of years, Sutton Town Hall has been virtually empty since April 1974, whilst City Departments occupy expensive premises within 100 yards of it, one of which is a modern dwellinghouse.

(b) In connection with Urban Renewal, even a minor project could involve three groups (or teams) five departments and six committees or sub-committees.

(c) I believe that the majority of officers are frustrated at their inability to operate efficiently. They have to refer matters to other persons or groups and not make up their own mind.

(d) I have had personal experience (and have had a number of complaints from my colleagues) that on numerous occasions when they try to 'phone an officer he is not available 'he is in a meeting'. This can only mean that time which should be spent on running a department is being frittered away in talking.

(e) The close working relationship between the Chairman of a committee and his Chief Officer was being broken down as incompatible with the corporate concept. I thought it was invaluable in the interests of the authority. It was from this that policy was often initiated and monitored and I considered this partnership of immense service to the City.

(f) Corporate Policy statements and Budgets have been presented and debated but I have yet to perceive their value in practice. Many people up and down the country now realise that Corporate Management, introduced as a tool of management aimed at greater co-ordination and the best use of resources has become something of a cult with its own dogma, priests and disciples. I have noted in reports such phrases as 'Corporate Management is a state of mind rather than a bundle of managerial techniques' and 'too many officers appear to lack a clear understanding of the philosophy of corporate working'. Comment is unnecessary.

(g) The Principal Chief Officers' Management Team has met weekly. Its agendas are voluminous and reports of 100 pages are not unusual. I find that many items do not provide firm recommendations and time is often spent on minor matters. This might not matter if it were a few juniors but the six or seven most highly paid officers, with three or four others in attendance have met regularly — an agenda had to be produced whether there was a difficult problem to be solved or not. Officers wasted time talking about or listening to matters of which they had no knowledge or experience and frankly with which they were not particularly concerned . . .

The structure introduced since 1974 does not, in my view suit Birmingham. In fact, the working group which produced the Bains Report included no-one working in such a large 'all purpose' authority as Birmingham. [Bosworth, 1976]

Following the Council's decision to rescind their support for a corporate approach a number of structural changes were made. These included the transfer of the central staff of policy analysts and research officers to the separate departments, a downgrading of the management team (and presumably of the policy committee) and, subsequently, the removal of the post of chief executive officer. The corporate machinery was disbanded.

Birmingham is not the only local authority that has reviewed and changed its organizational structure. Possibly the majority of authorities have reviewed their structures, and are still doing so, in the light of recent experiences. Many of the changes introduced after the Bains Report were comparatively novel, and it is not surprising that they have given rise to friction, and led to organizational adjustment. Some of the changes have been documented in earlier chapters. Not all of the changes, of course, are either as dramatic or as extensive as those of Birmingham. There have been a number of well-advertised changes, including the dismissal of several chief executive officers, and the resignation of directors of education. More usual, however, are the less publicized and less dramatic changes. For example, at Stockport and Bradford the numbers of interdepartmental groups have been reduced in order to rationalize their activities and to reduce the consumption of officers' time. At Leeds the size of the management team has been reduced from eight to three, and subsequently to four chief officers. A common change in the shire districts has been to amalgamate the responsibilities of the chief executive with those of the director of administration.

The internal details of these authorities are cited to illustrate that authorities throughout local government are expressing dissatisfaction with their structures, and are seeking improvements. In many cases the improvements made (or, more accurately, the structural changes believed to be improvements) move the authority concerned from one of the eight organizational patterns introduced in the previous chapter, to another. By considering and clarifying the role of the chief executive, and of the policy committee, an authority may move from a relatively deconcentrated to a concentrated pattern of integration.

How should the observer explain these structural movements? One approach would be to focus upon the role of key personalities (for example, Bosworth in the case of Birmingham) and trace the way in which structural change results from the interplay of strong and weak actors within the authority. Such an approach is widely cited throughout local government. From within any single authority the force and impact of personality is demonstrably visible and officers and members frequently express the importance of personalities. This is not surprising. People in organizations cannot fail to recognize and report the ability of individuals to shape events. And, there is documented evidence of the careers and achievements of powerful individuals (Dearlove, 1973; Donoughue and Jones, 1973; Elliott, 1971; Lee *et al.,* 1974; Sutcliffe, 1976; Sutcliffe and Smith, 1974; Skinner and Langdon, 1974; Wates, 1976). Contingency theory does not deride or deny the importance of individuals. The ability of individuals to shape the formal organizational structure of the local authority, and to influence the operation of that structure, has to be admitted. But there are other factors that may be important and it is upon these that contingency theory is focused. The numbers of committees and departments, the procedures that link and divide, the patterns of involvement and exclusion, cannot be seen entirely as the outcomes of individual actions unfettered by wider constraints. The roles of the chief executive and of the management team, the pattern of committees and departments, and the interactions between them may well reflect the dispositions of the individuals concerned; but they also reflect the organizational context within which they are set. The structure of the local authority is shaped by wider factors than that of personality.

Contingency theory asserts that these wider factors include characteristics of the authority such as its size, the range of its functions, and its political form. Contingency theory also asserts that characteristics of the environment, such as the configuration of problems, the availability of resources, and the pattern of demand articulation will determine organizational form. What is meant by these factors (size, political form and so on) and how they might shape the organization of a local authority, are questions developed in some detail in sections II and III below. It is worth elaborating a little further at this juncture, however, upon the wider character of contingency theory as a vehicle for the explanation of inter-authority variation and of organizational change.

The majority of officers and members would accept that the structures and procedures appropriate for Birmingham, or Liverpool, or Manchester, are unlikely to be those appropriate for the much smaller authorities of Brighton, Newark, or Congleton, even if these authorities had the same responsibilities. Few readers (if any) would disagree with this proposition. In other words, local authority *size* is widely accepted as an important contingency affecting the relevance of alternative local authority structures. Using the terminology discussed in Chapter 2, larger authorities can be expected to have to operate through comparatively extensive levels of differentiation. They will have more committees, sub-committees and departments than would be expected in smaller authorities.

A similar line of reasoning, which is perhaps equally non-contentious, is that the metropolitan districts will have more committees and departments than the shire districts. A metropolitan district, because of its wider range of responsibilities will have need of more committees and departments than a shire district of comparable size. Bristol shire district council, with a population of 422,000 can be expected to have less differentiation than (for example) Bradford metropolitan district, an authority serving a population of 463,000. The extent of structural variation will differ with the range of functions, despite similarities in size.

These are particular illustrations of how two 'contingencies' (size and range of functions) affect one aspect of organization (extent of differentiation). They serve to indicate why local authority structures vary: it is because of their different contextual circumstances. To explain why one authority differs from another, in other words, it is necessary to look at their situational circumstances. The variation observed in Chapters 3 and 4 is the product of variations in critical contingencies such as size and range of functions, and one way of explaining structural differences is to identify as many critical contingencies as possible, and to anticipate the direction of their impact.

Supposing however, that for some reason an authority has *not* adapted its structure to its critical contingencies: what then? What would be the consequences if an authority as large as Birmingham was not highly differentiated? It is in seeking an answer to this question that the emphasis moves towards a theory not of inter-authority variation, but of organizational change. Contingency theory would suggest that the development of inappropriate organizational arrangements (arrangements which fail to accommodate the exigencies of the situation) will lead to stresses and strains within the local authority that could only be reduced or removed by changing the structure until it is in line with the situational conditions. Stresses and strains might be of the form described above by Bosworth. In short, contingency theory would suggest that changes occurring in the structures of local authorities (such as those summarized in previous chapters) may be the consequence of stresses and strains within the organization created by the initial failure to properly match structures to situational contingencies. This, of course, is what Bosworth implies in his analysis of Birmingham when he says that 'the structure introduced since 1974 does not . . . suit Birmingham'.

Written in this way the impression given is that some local authorities made 'mistakes' in the design of their structures in 1973. This is probably a fair comment, although all changes cannot be attributed to earlier errors. But there are strong reasons for suspecting that many local authorities began their post-reorganization experience with inappropriate structures. In particular we would repeat our earlier remark that the recommendations of the Bains Working Group pushed many authorities to adopt structures not sufficiently tailored to local contingencies. This was hardly the Group's intention. Nevertheless, passages within their Report carried the imprint of universal relevance. For example:

> It is not our intention to lay down one structure which all authorities should adopt, but everything that has gone before in this report leads inevitably to certain basic structural features which we recommend should be common to all authorities. [p. 98]

Even those passages not intended for all authorities failed to work out the factors or contingencies that limit their relevance, and similarly failed (in most cases) to spell out alternatives. There are only limited and muted acknowledgements of two contingencies — size of authority and type (Long, 1975). Ironically, it was the simplicity of the Report which probably ensured its widespread attraction. Faced with the overwhelming complexities of local government reorganization, and the limited time in which it had to be achieved, local authorities found it expedient to follow many of the solutions preferred in that Report. Predictably, the structures are proving inappropriate to the contingencies faced by many authorities.

The purpose here is not to pillory the Bains Report, or to adopt a stance critical of the largely unquestioning response of local authorities to it. Given the circumstances under which the Study Group had to work, and the sometimes frenetic pace at which local authorities had to react, the position described above is understandable. The important point is that the Report, and the initial decisions of 1973, have left a structural legacy which cannot be ignored, namely, that many of the decisions on structure were inappropriate for the conditions facing many local authorities, and for this reason subsequent stresses and strains have provoked further organizational review and change.

At the outset of Reorganization, then, many local authorities probably had structures inconsistent with their situational contingencies, and it was predictable that, in these authorities, stresses and strains should appear. One push for organizational review, therefore, stemmed from the widespread adoption of inappropriate structures taken from the Bains Report. Birmingham, like many others, might rightly question whether Bains could 'suit' them, and whether it ever had. They might also question whether Bains (or whatever structures were set up in 1973) could suit them *now*. Circumstances have changed since 1974. Conditions are not the same as those operating when local authorities initially conceived their committee and departmental structures. Politically many authorities have changed party complexion, with the election results of 1974-6 sweeping away many Labour majorities and replacing them with even larger Conservative majorities. Authorities have to cope with different party majorities, increasing numbers of backbenchers, larger proportions of new and inexperienced members. Economically, too, circumstances have changed with the end of the conditions of growth which prevailed until 1974

(Wright, 1980). Local authorities are faced with pressure to curtail expenditure rather than to increase the provision of services.

As a result of changes in situational conditions local authorities may now find themselves structurally 'out of line'. The pattern of organization relevant to the conditions of 1973 may be inappropriate for the conditions of 1980. As a result stresses and strains will signal the need to reorganise internally. In explaining why Birmingham and others have felt the need to change reference has to be made to changing external conditions. Decisions made in 1973 may be the wrong decisions for 1980.

There are, then, at least two explanations for the processes of internal reorganization characteristic of many local authorities. One suggests that the original decisions on structure were inappropriate because they failed to take account of significant contingencies. As a consequence stresses and strains occur and provoke a review of the original decisions. (There is, of course, no guarantee that the subsequent decisions will be any better or more successful). The second explanation suggests that the original decisions were 'correct', in that structures were designed in line with local contingencies, but adds that the contingencies have changed creating the need for an organizational review. The latter explanation indicates that the need for organizational review and change might be a *persistent* one.

It should be clear from this discussion that contingency theory is a fertile approach to the explanation of existing structural arrangements, and to the explanation of structural change.

The kinds of variations summarized in Chapters 3 and 4 are partly caused by the different circumstances facing individual authorities. To understand that variation requires knowledge of the salient contingencies within the local government system, and of the consequences of those contingencies. Contingency theory also argues that changes such as those described above and those developed in previous chapters can also be traced to the attempts of local authorities to handle stresses and strains produced by an imperfect adjustment of structure to often changing situational contingencies.

Statements proclaiming that local authorities differ in their patterns of organization and management because they face different circumstances, or that those patterns change in response to changes in circumstances, are hardly exceptional. Many local government practitioners are quick to point to the need to design management systems and structures in the light of local conditions. By this is often meant the adaptation of structures to accommodate the strength of personalities. But, ironically, they often ignore their own words of wisdom and follow nationally dictated recommendations and fashions. The distinctive contribution of contingency theory, therefore, is not in the persuasive and sweeping claim that structures should fit local conditions, but in the systematic attempt to identify what *are* the important local conditions, and *what are their implications* for questions of organizational design. The following discussion attempts to answer these questions by reciting how various contingencies might be important for local government. These contingencies are of two forms: *environmental characteristics,* and *characteristics of the organization* itself.

Environmental Characteristics

It is frequently asserted within the literature of contingency theory that to understand the structures and performance of any organization some attention must be paid to the nature and form of its environment. The lengthy and sometimes repetitive line of theoretical debate and empirical reassessment prompted by the early, illuminating work of Burns and Stalker (1961) has amplified rather than diminished the importance of 'the environment' as a determinant of organizational form (Hage, 1978; Aldrich and Pfeffer, 1976; Aldrich, 1976). It is not from this literature, however, that we obtain an initial set of concepts with which to clarify the concept of the local authority's environment. On the contrary, a more useful point of departure for present purposes is offered by Boaden (1971).* Boaden's work leads to a conceptualization of the environment in terms of three elements:

*Boaden's work is situated within the confines of the 'socio-demographic' literature which seeks to explain policy outcomes (often equated with variations in expenditures) through analysis of environmental characteristics. Useful summaries and critiques of this approach are provided by Dearlove (1973, chapter 4) and Jenkins (1978, chapter 2). Readers interested in the conceptual distance between Boaden's initial work and the analysis developed here should refer to chapter 5 of Boaden's text and compare the discussion there with that presented above.

problems: the social, economic and physical characteristics
resources: the availability and supply of resources
demand articulation: the expression of preferences by groups
within the local community

The environment of the local authority, in other words, consists of
three parts. First, there are the social and economic conditions of
the client population, and the physical nature of the area within
which they reside and work. Authorities vary in the environmental
conditions with which they are faced. Some have decaying inner
cities, high levels of unemployment, significant areas of social
distress, and poor housing conditions. Some have extensive
agricultural lands, market towns rather than industrial cities, and
have declining populations. Others have disproportionate numbers
of certain social groups — the elderly, coloured immigrants, pre-
school children, and so on. The local authority has to respond to
its particular combination of environmental problems. It has to
organize itself in order to handle these problems. Not surprisingly,
therefore, authorities will have different management structures
and systems because they have different types and combinations
of problems. *In particular, we would expect that the greater the
range of substantial problems facing an authority the more
differentiated and integrated will be the appropriate form of
organization.*

Why should this be so? The increase in the size of many local
authorities in 1974 was regarded, in some quarters, as enabling
local government to obtain the benefits of economies of scale.
Larger populations would increase workloads to the point when
specialist skills could be recruited. For example, an authority
serving a large population will be required to make many decisions
concerned with land-use development and in making those
decisions may find it possible to employ specialist staff. The
workload generated by the large population warrants the employment of specialists. The authority may also find it convenient to
operate through committees and sub-committees solely concerned
with a specialized area. A high workload, in other words, (stemming
from a *substantial* environmental problem), will warrant the
separate organization and management of services that might
otherwise be administratively bundled together. Therefore, the
greater the number of these substantial environmental problems

and the bigger the authority, the greater will be the number of independent service committees and departments. That is, the range of substantial environmental problems affects the extent of differentiation.

The existence of many environmental problems will also affect the extent of integration. It was emphasized above that the act of structural differentiation, which is intended to reap the benefits of specialization, does so at the risk of fragmentation. Differentiation can lead to duplication, overlap and inconsistencies between policy areas. To avoid this risk an authority faced with multiple environmental problems may consider it advisable to increase the machinery of integration. In other words, the existence of multiple environmental problems will lead to an increase in the extent of differentiation which in turn will prompt the development of additional measures for overcoming fragmentation. The range of environmental problems in this way indirectly affects the level of structural integration. There may also be a direct effect. Authorities facing a cluster of problems may well be conscious of the complicated interactions that weave together social and economic problems. These authorities may recognize the need to tease out the multiple causes of environmental problems and may seek to understand the interrelated impacts of local services. It is these authorities, in other words, that may set up integrative structures because of their responsibility for several services within a context of multiple environmental problems.

The range of problems, then, may well be an important determinant of organizational form. So too might be the *types* of problems. Local authorities vary not only in terms of the numbers of problems with which they have to deal, but in the nature of those problems. The problems facing the older, industrialized, towns are not the same as those facing the modern generation of new towns. Similarly, coastal towns such as Blackpool and Brighton may not have the same difficulties as mining communities. Perhaps even more obviously a compact metropolitan district will have difficulties and environmental problems of a kind unfamiliar and less pressing to the sprawling counties. And yet, there may be examples from all these kinds of environments of authorities with the same number (range) of problems. To restrict attention to the range of environmental problems, therefore would be to miss an important feature of local authority environments, namely, the type of problems embodied within them.

It is not easy to specify in detail the kind of structures that might be associated with particular types of environmental problems. There are, it is true, a number of suggestions that might be advanced. For example, the older manufacturing areas might be expected to have structures that emphasize policy co-ordination. It is these areas that have often initiated extensive redevelopment of the physical infrastructure. And, from the need to co-ordinate the implementation of wide-ranging and complex capital schemes involving several departments, came machinery for interdepartmental and committee integration. The creation of structures for the integration of capital schemes is a short step from the creation of structures for the co-ordination of policy. Hence, the older, industrialized authorities, with their experience of co-ordination of land-use schemes, may well be those with extensive structures for the integration of policy. However, certain kinds of environment may well be associated with alternative structural forms and whether this is the case will be examined in later chapters. Detailed hypotheses will not be proposed.

The ability to respond to environmental conditions is at least partly dictated by the supply of resources. Finance, skilled manpower, the availability of land and premises, these and other resources affect the ability of local authorities to detect and treat problems in the environment. The availability of resources provides an opportunity to act: the lack of resources serves as a constraint. To suggest that the relative availability of resources is an important contingency acting upon organizations is not contentious, even though it has been largely ignored in the literature (there are exceptions to this: Benson, 1975; Aldrich, 1976; Zald, 1970). In elaborating the idea further, however, and in tracing the likely impact of resource availability upon structures, an important distinction must be made. On the one hand there are inter-authority variations in *absolute wealth*. Some authorities are able to raise resources from the local population with comparative ease. There may be industrial premises and domestic households that yield substantial financial income. These may be attractive social, educational and cultural amenities which attract and retain professional employees (compare, for example, the magnetic pull of London with that of other, more depressed, regions). They may have extensive tracts of land available for development. These authorities, set within an environment containing a ready and substantial pool of resources, are wealthy in an absolute sense.

Wealthy authorities will be more differentiated, less integrated, and will employ a more deconcentrated style of integration than authorities with less resources. The existence of environmental problems in a wealthy authority can be handled through the generation and allocation of resources to appropriate services. Wealth allows a local authority to respond. It affords the employment of specialist staff and the creation of separate groups, or departments, each directed at an environmental problem. Each will report to a committee or sub-committee. The costs of employing such staff in sufficient numbers to warrant their organization as a separate section or department is less problematical to the wealthier authority than it is to the less wealthy. Hence, wealth may support structural differentiation. Wealthy authorities will also be less concerned with the costs of co-ordination. Financial pressures focus attention upon the administrative costs of duplication and overlap. The tighter the financial situation, the more conscious will the authority be of the need to prevent any waste of resources caused by lack of co-ordination both in policy formulation and administrative implementation. Wealth, in contrast, lessens the pressure for integration.

At least *some* structural integration will occur, however, in all authorities. Wealthy authorities still seek to be efficient even if the spur is less sharp. We might expect as a consequence that the style of integration in wealthy authorities will differ from that in poorer authorities. In particular, the former will be less concentrated. The build-up of strong central units characteristic of a concentrated style of integration can often be (in part) a response to scarcity of resources. The lack of sufficient resources to support the employment of specialist staffs such as corporate planners, research officers, or personnel officers, in *several* departments leads to the location of those functions in a central department. Wealthier authorities, on the other hand, have sufficient resources to deploy these functions throughout the service departments. Similarly, wealthy authorities can afford the time and effort required to staff a network of corporate groups, which is a second characteristic of a deconcentrated integrative style. Departments in these authorities will have sufficient staff to meet the demands of attending and preparing for group meetings. Authorities with slender resources are less able to support a network of corporate groups and are more likely to have a small number of specialist staff under the chief executive. Wealth supports a deconcentrated style of integration.

The existence of absolute wealth is one of the important characteristics of the resource environment. A second is the relative *stability* of the resource supply. Irrespective of absolute wealth, changes in the availability of resources, especially if those changes are of an unpredictable form, can be equally important for the design of committee and departmental structures. It is this aspect of the resource environment, moreover, which has become increasingly important in recent years. The rate of inflation in the United Kingdom since 1974 has been one of the highest amongst western industrial societies. A consequence has been an economic strategy intended to reduce the level of public expenditure and, as part of a wider attempt to switch resources from public to manufacturing sectors, reduce the proportion of GNP going into the public sector. Control of local government expenditure was regarded as crucially important for the successful implementation of this new strategy. To achieve that control a series of circulars were disseminated by central government delineating the worsening economic circumstances, outlining their implications for local government expenditure, and exhorting local authorities to achieve substantial reductions in both anticipated and committed expenditure.

Central government did not rely solely upon the arguments and exhortations laid out in the succession of White Papers and circulars. Sanctions were applied. For example, Circular 88/75 (Local Authority Expenditure in 1976/77 — Forward Planning), which detailed the necessity of a standstill in expenditure, was reinforced in two ways. The Rate Support Grant Settlement for that year was calculated from the basis of a standstill, that is, it made nil allowance for committed or further expenditure. Secondly, the Settlement introduced cash limits on the size of the Grant and of subsequent Increase Orders, thus facing local authorities with the option of complying with Circular 88/75, or of raising additional resources through local taxation. In the following year additional sanctions were imposed. In particular, the Rate Support Settlement 1977/78 reduced the amount of local government expenditure to be met from the Grant from 65.5 to 61 per cent. In other words, the three budgetary years from 1974-5 were marked by a *relatively rapid* deterioration in the supply of resources made available to local authorities, a deterioration that made it difficult for authorities to predict the amount of grant that would be forthcoming. For example:

> In 1975/76, the errors in predicting grant income were large. For the shire counties, they ranged from −22.2 to +15.6 percent, for the metropolitan districts from −22.4 to +13.8 percent, and for the London boroughs from −22.6 to −1.0 percent. [Lynch and Perlman 1978, p. 19]

The magnitude of these errors may have been unduly large in 1975/6. Lynch and Perlman found that errors in the following years were of a more modest scale. Nevertheless, it is clear that in recent years local authorities have had to cope with uncertainties in the resource environment caused by the unpredictable decisions of central government concerning the *level* of the Rate Support Grant. Some authorities, however, have suffered from rather more uncertainty than have others. It has not only been changes in the level of Grant which has perplexed local authorities but changes in the procedures for *allocating* the Grant between authorities. Jackman and Sellars, reviewing these changes, summarized the situation as follows:

> The new procedure for needs grant distribution has been a source of continued concern and dissatisfaction to local authorities. Variables have been introduced into the formula which have no clear relevance to local government services. Some variables seem to have appeared and disappeared in a somewhat haphazard fashion, while the weights given to others have seemed excessively volatile from one year to the next. Despite efforts to stabilise the distribution, *the relative amounts of grant going to individual authorities have varied considerably from year to year.* [1977, p. 19, emphasis added]

In other words, since 1974 an important contingency within the environment of the local authority has been the degree of uncertainty or instability of the supply of resources. We would expect resource uncertainty, as reflected in unpredictable changes in grant received, to affect the relevance of alternative organizational arrangements. *In particular we would expect a high rate of instability to result in lower differentiation, but to be associated with* higher or lower *integration, and* more or less *concentration.*

The arguments to do with resource instability (as experienced over the past few years) and structural differentiation are very close to those described in relation to absolute wealth. That is, authorities faced with declining resources, and uncertainty about the likely supply of future resources, will be unable to finance extensive differentiation. Faced with falling resources and the need for cuts in expenditure the organization itself becomes the target for saving. Labour-intensive organizations such as local authorities will inevitably seek savings through the control and reduction of manpower. Savings will also be sought through rationalization of committee and sub-committee structures in order to curb the administrative expense of servicing a large number of separate units. Falling supplies of resources, in short, will lead to falling structural differentiation. It is unlikely, however, that this effect will occur quickly. Authorities have to await opportunities afforded by retirements of senior officers, or their resignation, before departments are dissolved. Similarly, it is not always easy to disband committees in the face of resistance from senior councillors reluctant to lose the status and influence associated with the role of committee chairman. Nevertheless, over several years falling resources may well lead to reduced differentiation.

Much more immediate effects may be expected upon the level of integration. There are two possibilities. On the one hand, resource instability may lead to a growth in machinery of integration and the development of a concentrated style. It has already been proposed that lack of resources has the effect of accentuating demands for efficiency and the removal of policy waste and inconsistencies. These demands are expressed through the creation of integrative structures set up to avoid organizational fragmentation. It may also be that organizations in situations of crisis react by tightening control over strategic decisions (Chandler, 1962; Sloan, 1965). Hence unstable and falling resources may lead local authorities to institute more, and concentrated, integrative structures. An alternative argument is that the authority will seek savings through dismemberment of the corporate machinery (as in Birmingham). Earlier, reference was made to 'politically' inspired retreats from corporate management, aimed at securing efficiency and economy. Savings were achieved by dismissing the chief executive, limiting the role of the management team, abolishing corporate groups and so forth. In these authorities the corporate machinery is itself a target for saving, rather than a means of obtaining savings through the pursuit of co-ordination. This line of argument provides the hypothesis that falling resources will be associated with lower structural integration.

The third element of the local authority environment is the pattern of demand articulation. Local authorities are made aware of certain environmental problems through their own 'search' procedures. Departments carry out research into the conditions and circumstances of the population. In some cases surveys are fundamental to the work of the department, and sometimes they are required by central government departments. From these surveys and similar search procedures the local authority learns about the environment. But the environment is not passive or indifferent to the activities of the authority. Groups within the environment will mobilize both to raise issues with the council and to persuade the council of the necessary steps that should be taken. For example, Wates (1976) has chronicled the attempts of a group of residents in the Tolmers Square area of Camden to put their case forcibly to the Council. Saunders (1974) and Elkin (1974) have mapped links between large corporations and council activities. These are examples of affected parties putting their case to the council and seeking favourable policy outcomes. In some instances the council is receptive to the ideas thrust upon it and acts accordingly (Saunders, 1974). In others the authority is much less responsive (Davies, 1972; Dearlove, 1973).

We would expect the organization of the local authority to be affected by the pattern of expressed demands. If demands are extensive, for example, stressing the need for responses to a range of problems, and the need, and requirements of many client groups, the effect will be to articulate the pressures created by multiple environmental problems. That is, they will increase the tendency towards differentiation. Furthermore, demands pressed upon the local authority may point to inadequate co-ordination of existing policies and services, or the need for new policy directions. For example, various experiments conducted in recent years (such as community development projects) have highlighted problems that do not fit neatly into traditional service structures. These experiments have called for new mechanisms for policy co-ordination in order to tackle the problems of deprivation and disadvantage (Stewart *et al.,* 1976; Corina, 1977). Authorities which have experienced these kinds of experiments may well find it convenient to develop additional integrative structures.

Demand articulation is clearly important. Having admitted that, however, we are unable to pursue the matter further within the present research framework. The considerable range and type of groups acting upon local authorities (Newton, 1976) makes it impossible to devise simple measures to pick up the differences between authorities. There is no available way of measuring and comparing the demand environments of local authorities. Thus, in examining the effects of environment upon local authority organizational arrangements, the present study does not provide data on the importance of demand articulation.

ORGANIZATIONAL CHARACTERISTICS

It is not only factors within the environment that determine the relevance of alternative structures. The character of the organization itself is important. This section lists those factors that have been of theoretical significance elsewhere and which promise some contribution to knowledge and understanding of local authorities. Not all the organizational characteristics considered in the literature of contingency theory will be discussed. Many are irrelevant to the study of local government. Two, however, figure prominently in the literature and have a clear relevance for local government:

organizational size
technology

Both of these are organizational characteristics that have been studied extensively and yielded promising results. A third organizational characteristic is much more rarely found within published contingency studies, although it may well have significant explanatory force. This is

public accountability

Interestingly, not one of the major contributions to contingency theory has considered the existence of elected representatives, to whom an organization is subordinated and who are themselves accountable to a wide electorate, as a significant contingency operating upon government bureaucracies. Despite the wide variety of studies carried out into *public* organizations (Blau, 1968; Meyer,

1972; Hage and Aiken, 1967, 1969; Hall, 1962, 1963) contingencies such as organizational size and the nature of production technologies are treated as the salient variables. The impact of public accountability is either ignored or treated as insignificant. The status of public accountability within organizational analysis, in other words, contrasts with the treatment given it within political science when it receives considerable attention (Self, 1972; Ridley, 1975). As argued in Chapter 1 it is important to take into account the fact that local authorities are political institutions. Consequently some attempt must be made to examine the likely effect of political factors upon organizational arrangements.

Organizational Size

The impacts of size are not easily separated from the impacts of environment. We have already hypothesized that an authority faced with extensive and complex problems within the environment will respond by setting up additional sub-committees and committees, and by employing specialists to deal with such functions as research and intelligence. These increases in differentiation would create difficulties of co-ordination necessitating the creation of additional integrative arrangements. It was also hypothesized that the existence of several problems in the environment would prompt an attempt at integrated policy formulation (see Figure 5.1).

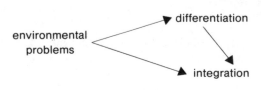

FIGURE 5.1

The effects of organizational size are not dissimilar. Local authorities need not respond fully to environmental problems. Indeed, it is probable that they cannot respond to all problems because of insufficient resources, or because there is a lack of appreciation about how an authority should respond. The decline of the inner cities, imbalanced industrial infrastructures, rising instances of juvenile crime, are examples of problems that cannot be treated exhaustively. Local authorities do not *know* how to respond, and do not have the resources to do so. Authorities may also lack the political will ('disposition') to respond. What is important is that the extent to which a local authority responds will partly show through in the size of the organization (numbers of employees and the amount of capital and revenue expenditures). For example, an authority which seeks a comprehensive response to the various social problems within its area can be expected to employ more social workers, provide more facilities such as meals on wheels, provide more home helps, and so on, than an authority which undertakes more limited response to the same problems.

In other words, authorities can vary in size even though their environments are similar. And, larger authorities (that is those with greater numbers of employees) will have particular organizational problems. In particular, *size will lead to greater measures of structural differentiation and of integration. There might also be a tendency towards a deconcentrated style.*

These effects will occur for similar reasons to those put forward in discussing the effects of environmental problems. The larger local authority, because it has chosen to handle a greater volume of business, will have to take more decisions, provide more services, employ more staff, and perform more activities. Increases of this kind warrant the creation of separate sub-committees and departmental sections for functions previously administered together. For example, the social services committee may splinter into sub-committees handling the problems of the aged, or pre-school children, or for geographical areas of the authority. The same authorities may also find it appropriate to employ new skills. A large organization will justify sections specializing in personnel, or public relations, or research and intelligence and so on. Similarly, a high volume of business could justify a department of administration separate from the chief executive. In other words, a larger local authority warrants greater differentiation.

These opportunities for differentiation, if taken, lead to increases in problems of control, communication and co-ordination. The more an organization is broken into separate parts the greater the risk of fragmentation. There are at least two reasons for this. There is the sheer administrative complexity of making sure that departments and committees are aware both of what others are doing, and of the implications of their own activities for those carried out elsewhere. It is much more difficult within a large organization to *comprehend* the interactions and exchanges necessary to avoid inefficiencies such as duplication of work, and slowness of response to requests from other departments. There is also the tendency towards 'departmentalism'. A major stumbling block to co-ordination can be the apparent *unwillingness* of personnel within different parts of the organization to interact and co-operate. An inevitable consequence of structural differentiation is the creation of loyalties and commitments to departments and committees rather than to the organization as a whole. This, of course, was central for the analysis of the Committee on Management (1967) and has informed the majority of studies into the management of local government. It should be recognized, however, that this is not a characteristic of public organizations alone, but is endemic to all large-scale organizations (see the works of Strauss (1962), Landsberger (1961), Walton and Dutton (1969), and more recently, of Pettigrew (1973), Baldridge (1971), and Burns (1977)). The second consequence of size, in short, is the need for additional structures directed at policy co-ordination.

There is extensive evidence from the literature of contingency theory supporting the theoretical association of size with increases of structural integration. Pugh *et al.* (1969), Child (1973), Blau and Schoenherr (1971), and Heydebrand (1973) and others all find support for this proposition. Parodoxically, the authors of one of the few studies available from the literature of public administration claim that their researches do *not* support the proposition. Long and Richer (1968) concluded from a study of four types of departments in thirty-three English county boroughs that

> Apart from the decentralisation of services (i.e. maintenance of district or area officers physically separate from a central head office) we found little evidence that large authorities make special adaptations in organization for the purpose of coping with the problem of scale . . . Formal arrangements aimed at co-ordination within and between departments at officer level seem to be little more extensive than in smaller authorities. [p. 61]

There is some doubt whether the authors have correctly interpreted their material. There are several references that run counter to their conclusion. For example:

> Further confirming the impression that . . . larger authorities rely on more formal methods of contact, we found that larger authorities

think that circulars and memoranda are more important than they are considered to be in similar county boroughs. [p. 31]

And

Generally speaking it appears that there is a tendency for methods of co-ordination to become more formalised in the larger authorities. [p. 39]

Given the considerable evidence from the organizational literature for our hypothesis, coupled with the debatable status of the evidence from Long and Richer there is sufficient justification for asserting that local authority size will be associated with the extent of structural integration.

The *style* of integration that might accompany local authority growth is less easy to predict. One possibility, proposed by Blau (1968) is that organizations will become less centralized (in our terms, less concentrated). Blau suggests that concentrated structures are more appropriate in smaller organizations where co-ordination can be achieved through face-to-face interaction. In the local authority context any attempts to route all items from service departments and committees through the policy committee, and the management team becomes increasingly unworkable as the numbers of service areas expands. A concentrated style of integration is possible only where service committees and departments are limited in numbers.

There is an alternative thesis. One of the consequences of local authority growth, as noted above, is that the workload justifies the appointment of functional specialists. For example, larger local authorities are developing more and more specialists such as cororate planners, research officers, personnel officers and estate officers to introduce and develop policy and resource co-ordination. These experts are located *at the centre* of the local authority and will seek to concentrate the lines of reporting and accountability. They introduce controls over the service departments, weaving a more concentrated pattern of integration. In other words, the style of integration within the larger local authorities is likely to be concentrated, rather than deconcentrated.

There are, then, contradictory conclusions implied by the exigencies of growth. On the one hand, size provides the opportunities for structural differentiation and the associated advantages of specialization. On the other it accentuates the difficulties of co-ordination and control and increases the need for machinery to attain structural integration. *Larger local authorities will, therefore, be associated with a greater extent of differentiation (more committees, sub-committees and departments) and of integration (greater use of policy and resource committees, corporate groups, functional specialists, etc.). The style of integration that will be found in these authorities is less clear. It could either be concentrated or deconcentrated.*

Technology (Type of Authority)

It is almost a working assumption of local government that the practices of alternative types of authority differ significantly. Reports are often prepared and data presented by type of authority. Local government officers often regard themselves as 'county men', or 'metro men', and see their careers within one type of local authority. There are some indications that this division between county and metropolitan areas is less than that which separated county from county boroughs, but movement within one type of authority is still the prevalent pattern. But why should there be significant differences between, say, a metropolitan district and a county authority? What implicit dimension are we attempting to understand when type of authority is put forward as an influential contingency?

A familiar notion within contingency theory is that the technology employed by an organization may be an important factor determining the appropriateness of structural form. It is probably the most widely canvassed 'contingency' found in the literature. Numerous writers have sought to clarify and test the idea of a technological imperative. It is, however, a difficult idea to grasp and develop because it has been used in a variety of ways both conceptually and empirically. The confusion is aptly illustrated by Perrow who, commenting upon the original work by Joan Woodward (1958, 1965), objected that Woodward's definition of technology 'is not, strictly speaking technology, but is a mixture of production, size of production run, layout of work and type of customer order' (1967). Nevertheless, from the available material at least two schools may be identified.

One sub-school centres around the influence of machine technologies upon the organization. This line of inquiry can be directly traced to Woodward's approach. Some of the authors within this group have examined the impact of technology upon the behaviour and attitudes of employees (Blauner, 1964; Faunce, 1968; Walker and Guest, 1952) although, even in these instances, reference is frequently made to the structures associated with different technologies. Also in this tradition are those who have looked at the impact of computers (Whisler, 1970; Schoderbek, 1971). The common argument of these writers is that different machine technologies have unique effects upon the division of labour (extent of differentiation) and therefore upon the problems of co-ordination and employee commitment. The extents of differentiation and integration can therefore be expected to vary according to the technology used. The evidence for this argument is sketchy. Woodward (1965) and Zwerman (1970) do provide support but of a crude form: in particular, their operational measures of technology are not always clear. More impressive evidence is provided by Hickson *et al.* (1969) but tends to run counter to the idea that machine technologies are a principal determinant of structures.

The second sub-school focusses upon the concept of routineness or uniformity. Theoretically (Litwak, 1961; Perrow, 1967) and empirically (Burns and Stalker, 1961; Lawrence and Lorsch, 1967; Hage and Aiken, 1969) it has been noted that organizations vary in the degree of unpredictability faced in performance of productive tasks, and that the extent of task unpredictability may influence the form of organization. Results within this tradition consistently associate task predictability with highly structured forms of organization.

In one sense the study of technology is impressive for the sheer variety of approaches and the ingenuity demonstrated in the definition and identification of concepts and associations. The overriding conclusion, however, must be that the status of technology as a determinant of structure is uncertain and disputed. The results obtained are inconsistent and seem to depend as much on the initial choice of measures as the conceptual argument. Nevertheless the hypothesis that choice of technology will affect the administrative structure does have some theoretical attraction and we are reluctant to discard it from our analysis. The problem is to discover appropriate starting points from the confusing wealth of published research and suggestion.

There are, in fact, a number of hints that may assist. In particular, Anderson and Warkov (1961) in a study of hospitals suggest that the greater the number of tasks the greater the problems of co-ordination and control. In other words, it is range of functions, or functional diversity that is the important dimension; and, in considering type of authority we shall be testing the impact of functional diversity. The greater the functional diversity as indicated by the range of functions, then the greater may be both the differentiation (in order to cope with the larger number of tasks) and the integration (to pull the several tasks together) of the authority.

The intention, in other words, is to consider type of authority as a shorthand for a particular aspect of technology, namely, *functional diversity*. To think of type of authority in this way is to make a number of assumptions. For example, no account is taken of the complexity *within* individual services. More importantly, perhaps, there is the assumption that local authorities are equally aware of the need for policy co-ordination, and are inclined to meet that need. There is little reason to doubt that the greater the range of functions the more likely it is that an authority will operate through larger numbers of committees and departments. This part of the hypothesis is unexceptionable. But it is less easy to accept unquestioningly that functional diversity will lead to greater structural integration. Admittedly, the larger number of interactions operated will probably require additional arrangements for interdepartmental co-ordination, in much the same way as that described above for the question of organizational size. Nevertheless, there is evidence from previous studies (see Chapter 4) that many local authorities are prepared to allow service committees and departments to operate in relative independence from each other, and are not necessarily inclined to seek policy co-ordination. Responsibility for many functions need not lead to attempts at policy co-ordination. Therefore, it is strictly inaccurate to anticipate that metropolitan districts *as a type* will have more structural integration than the shire districts purely on the grounds that the latter have fewer functions. There may well be certain shire districts deeply committed to the pursuit of policy co-ordination irrespective of their narrower range of functions. There may also be large metropolitan authorities uncommitted to it. Nevertheless, in general authorities with the greater range of functions will have more need of, and will seek, more formalized arrangements for policy co-ordination. Although the assumption underlying the latter part of the hypothesis is debatable, the idea of task affecting structure is none the less worth further examination.

Public Accountability

The contingencies discussed so far are commonly found within the organizational literature. They figure extensively in the relevant journals and have been both conceptually honed and repeatedly tested in a variety of settings. Public accountability, on the other hand, is remarkable for its absence in the same literature. There have been few attempts to explicate the effects of different forms of ownership and control upon the structures and procedures of organization. And yet, it would not appear unreasonable to expect government bureaucracies to be different from their non-public counterparts. Government bureaucracies are required to meet political pressures rather more than the pressures of economics. Manufacturing organizations, on the other hand, seek to meet economic criteria of success. Thus, Woodward defined success as

> profitability, market standing, rate of development and future plans . . . the volume of the industry's output, the proportion of that volume produced by the firm concerned and the nature of the market . . . [p. 59 in Pugh, 1971]

Similarly, Lawrence and Lorsch (1967) used

> . . . three performance measures; change in profits over the past five years; change in sales volume over the past five years; and new products introduced in the past five years as a percent of current sales . . . [p. 39]

These definitions of success, or effectiveness, are *economic* definitions. They are relevant for organizations operating within an economic context.* Local authorities, however, operate where

---

*This is not to ignore, however, that many non-public organizations seek to *control* (rather than simply adapt to) their environment, thus avoiding the need to be structured according to the prevailing contingencies. Examples of organizations controlling their environments are provided by Franko (1974) and McNeil (1978).

considerations other than economic factors may be given a higher importance. Organizational success is not assessed by economic criteria and the structural arrangements required may not be those dictated by economic contingencies. Roy Jenkins, comparing his experiences in the Home Office and the Treasury, illustrates the point:

> The old Home Office system, although exclusive, did not appear to me to produce a totally self-confident outlook. The Department, although not anxious to change, was uncertain about its place in the world. There was a slightly defensive expectation that whenever the Home Office attracted public attention it would also attract public blame. I remember seeing a sympathetic and semi-jocular minute written by one of my predecessors. 'Poor old Home Office', it ran, 'we are occasionally right, but we always get the blame'. That struck me as depressing.
>
> The Treasury, as I knew it, was more self-confident, less centralized, more relaxed. It operated upon the basis of easy informality. Christian names were always used. All my private secretaries automatically called the Permanent Secretary by his. There was never the slightest difficulty in provoking argument and disagreement at meetings. Most people had plenty to say, and didn't mind to whom they said it, or whether the recipient of their views agreed with them or not.
>
> At the same time, a great number of things were decided and done at a comparatively low level. Draft answers to Parliamentary Questions, for example, rarely went above Assistant Secretary level before being submitted to Ministers. In the Home Office they nearly all went to the Permanent Secretary. Much the same applied to the briefing for Cabinet meetings and Committees. Senior officials were interested in advising on major policy, not in preventing Ministers making fools of themselves. If they couldn't avoid this with the help of an Assistant Secretary, either the Minister or the Assistant Secretary, or both, oughtn't to be in the Treasury at all . . .
>
> The Treasury does not require the same meticulous standards of detailed administration. It deals little with the public. A lot of the work turns more on giving opinions, often somewhat by-and-large opinions, than on making or recommending decisions. And opinions can rarely be absolutely right or wrong, or at any rate cannot be proved to be so. Judgement and originality are often more important than accuracy and knowledge.
>
> This does not apply to the Home Office. When I became Home Secretary it was only one year free of the death penalty. This sombre institution had to some extent pervaded the whole atmosphere. The Secretary of State's room was hardly made gayer by the presence, even if the discreetly concealed presence, of a board adjusted from day to day and recording the imminence of all pending executions.

The responsibility for making recommendations as to what should be done in these cases weighed heavily upon all the officials concerned.

Such a duty could only be discharged by sensitive men if attempted with a clinically strict regard for precedent and consistency. This affected the approach to other cases dealt with in the Criminal Department, and persisted after the death penalty itself had disappeared. It is indeed necessary in cases involving the decisive exercise of executive power over individuals even if the dreadful finality of an execution is absent. The use of the prerogative of mercy in relation to prison sentences or decisions about deportation must have a defensible pattern of consistency. Otherwise there would be an intolerable sense of arbitrariness . . .

Meticulous and precise administration is therefore an essential part of the Home Office tradition, and with it, as the reverse side of the same coin, tends to go a certain rigidity of outlook. (Jenkins, 1971).

Jenkins is clearly writing of organizations operating in contexts different from those described by Woodward, and Lawrence and Lorsch. Whereas the one set of organizations strive for performance measured ultimately in economic terms, governmental organizations, including local authorities, have to balance the pressures for economy with pressures of a non-economic form derived from their political framework. As Dunsire (1973) puts it:

. . . public administration is not merely allowed to 'get results', it must stay within the law, achieve fairness or equity, conduct its affairs with utter financial and moral probity, behave correctly at all times and in all circumstances. [p. 169]

We are not suggesting that non-governmental organizations pursue economic goals to the complete exclusion of other 'goals'. But there are strong reasons for suggesting that political goals will exert a stronger influence in public agencies. Firstly, the political framework is institutionalized, making it legitimate to subordinate economic goals and economic criteria for success in favour of political goals and political criteria. It is unlikely that a Labour Party would put aside schemes for a 'comprehensive' system of secondary education purely on grounds of the costs of such schemes compared to the costs of alternative schemes, although costs will not be ignored in consideration of such issues (Hampton, 1970, p. 276). Similarly, the proposals for joint planning staffs for the new two-tier system of local government were abandoned in favour of proposals for each authority to have its own planning complement, thus meeting the political factors of the county-district system at the expense of economic considerations. The extent to which the conflict between economic and political considerations is institutionalized and therefore legitimated within the machinery of government, is indicated by the deliberate design of the public corporation as a vehicle that would not too easily subordinate economic to political requirements (Ostergaard, 1954; Tivey, 1966).

Secondly, public organizations are not faced with the same kind of economic forces: the 'invisible hand' of the market does not impinge quite so acutely. Private organizations face a much greater need to remain economically viable. Not to do so would threaten the very existence of the enterprise. Public organizations on the other hand are not dependent upon the open market for revenue: public funds are usually secured primarily from taxation. Local authorities receive almost two-thirds of their income either from local taxation sources (rates) or from grants from the government. A considerable proportion of the remaining income is from rents. Only a tiny fraction of local resources, in short, is subject to consumer inclination. Given this steady income, the pressures upon the local authority to be 'efficient' are not as acute as in private industry, although this is less true for recent years during which the financial pressures have become much more restrictive. This is, moreover, especially the case when one considers that the local authority not only receives revenue divorced from consumer inclination, but is able to isolate itself from its immediate environment. Thus, for some local services there are few, if any, alternative services provided by competitors that would indicate consumer preference. For other services there is considerable demand for *existing* services, making consideration of alternative services unnecessary. For some services there is compulsory consumption. These conditions are unlikely to push the local authority into making economic viability of *critical* importance in the allocation of resources.

Recognition of the importance of political considerations is an essential but first step. There is a need to clarify what we mean by political pressures: what, in short, is to be understood by the idea of a political contingency. There are at least two aspects of the political context important for the design of organizational structures. Firstly, there is the degree to which councillors formally organize themselves into identifiable political groupings: this is the extent of *political organization* (Greenwood and Hinings, 1976; Greenwood, 1978). Secondly, there is the *complexion* of the controlling political party: whether it is Labour, Conservative, or some other party.

The degree to which local authority councillors are organized politically varies between authorities. At one extreme are authorities such as those described by Jennings (1975) in which elected representatives are not aligned into cohesive factions. Political 'parties' in these authorities lack 'common' perspectives or agreements over a broad range of issues, although more fluid, temporary coalitions of representatives may emerge for particular issues. At the other extreme the council may consist of competing, highly organized groups, each with a set of values which it attempts to embody in the policies and decisions of the government. Such parties take responsibility for the affairs of the authority, controlling both the distribution of patronage (which enables the party to capture the administrative apparatus) and the behaviour of their own members in operating that apparatus. Examples of such authorities are provided by Bulpitt (1967), Dearlove (1973), Elliott (1975), Jones (1973), Wiseman (1963), Sutcliffe (1976) and Newton (1976). The majority of local authorities fall somewhere between these extremes (Rhodes, 1975) although there has been a tendency since the 1974 Reorganization towards increases in political organization. The amalgamation of previously separate county boroughs characterized by highly organized parties, with the more loosely structured shire counties, has led an increasing proportion of authorities to assume more stringent forms of party organization.

We would expect authorities characterized by highly organized political parties to have distinctive structural properties. *In particular, they will have a concentrated style of integration.* Highly organized political parties are hierarchical in form. They have a party leader and a caucus of senior politicians. The party group, through the caucus, will use the policy committee and its sub-committee as the central instruments through which strategic decisions are taken on resource allocation and policy priorities. Party groups will recognize the correspondence between the structural requirements of party control, and the organizational consequences of corporate planning. Consider, for example, the place of the policy committee. The policy committee was introduced into local government largely as a vehicle for corporate planning. It is part of the administrative machinery through which policy co-ordination was to be secured. From a political standpoint, however, the policy committee offers the party caucus a means of effecting political control. The policy committee allows the party hierarchy to structure and control the *formal* processes of decision-making within the authority, thus complementing its control over activities that occur behind the scenes. Consider also the position of the chief executive officer. The political leadership within an increasingly organized party will find it advantageous to build up the roles of the chief executive officer, and (to a lesser extent) of the management team. Highly organized parties, attempting at least some control and co-ordination over the policies of service committees and departments, will turn to the officer structure for an alternative source of information to that offered by the departmental chief officer. A central policy committee will find it easier to break the centrifugal influence of the committee-chief officer link if information is channelled through central officers who see their role in authority-wide terms, and not as advocates for the expansion of professional services. The leadership of a highly organized party, in other words, will find it convenient to operate through a policy committee supported by an officer structure characterized by a concentrated routing of information and reporting.

The extent of political organization affects the organization of a local authority irrespective of which political party is in control. It does not matter for the above analysis whether it is a Conservative or Labour party which dominates the authority: the style of integration will be influenced by the internal organization of the party. This is not to argue that the complexion of the council is unimportant. On the contrary, we expect the practices of Labour authorities to differ from those found within Conservative authorities, but these effects should be seen as independent from those caused by the degree of political organization. The effects of party control upon organizational structure have been little studied in the United Kingdom. There are, however, two suggestions. Greenwood and Stewart (1973) have suggested that the Labour Party is much more likely to embrace the ideas of corporate planning and policy co-ordination. Labour-controlled authorities are more receptive to techniques and approaches directed at the planning of services as a programmed response to environmental conditions. Conservative authorities, on the other hand, are less interested in exploring the links between services, and the combined impacts of several services upon the local community. The philosophy of the Conservative Party is to treat local authorities as responsible for the administration of a discrete range of services, rather than for the government of a community. The Conservative Party is, therefore, much less likely to adopt the ideas of corporate planning. The Labour Party, on the other hand, may find those ideas more attractive because of its ideological sympathy with social and economic planning. If this hypothesis is correct then Labour-controlled authorities can be expected to have the greater extents of structural integration. Conservative authorities, on the other hand, will have a more modest array of policy committees and integrative departments.

A second line of reasoning is provided by the Committee on Management (1967). The Committee's research found that Labour-controlled administrations pay more attention to detail at committee level. Assuming that the consideration of detail adds to the length and frequency of committee meetings, there will be pressures for larger numbers of committees and sub-committees in order to make the transaction of business on any single committee more manageable. In short, Labour-controlled authorities will have highly differentiated committee structures. Given the strong tendency for professionals to seek direct access to elected representatives, coupled with the inclination of members to prefer their 'own' chief officer, there may also be a tendency for Labour-controlled authorities to have higher rates of officer differentiation.

The effects of party complexion, therefore, will be as follows. *Labour authorities will make more use of integrative structures, because of their commitment to forms of policy planning; and, they will have more committees and departments, because of their greater concern with the details of committee businesss.*

SUMMARY

Local authorities are faced with an array of contingent circumstances which determine the relevance of alternative structural arrangements. These contingencies are of two forms: those to do with the environment (resources, needs, demands) and those to do with characteristics of the organization itself. Each of the contingencies has (or might be expected to have) independent impacts upon organizational structures. The conceptual framework as it has been described promises to provide some explanation of why local authority structures vary. Because local authorities face varying circumstances they require, and will adopt, different structures. Some authorities face the problems of organizational size, whereas others do not. Some are set within wealthy environments, others are not. These differences can be expected to have importance influences upon the choice of structure.

How far these expectations are correct will be examined in the next chapter. We shall consider the contingencies identified and discussed in this chapter and trace their separate impact upon local authority structures. We shall also consider (in Chapter 7) the relationship between the contingencies, and their *combined* effect upon structure. Our discussion in this chapter may well have suggested that disparate contingencies act in isolation. This is, of course, untrue. As well as directly influencing the shape of a local authority's structure each contingency frequently mediates the impact of another. The task of Chapter 7 will be to make explicit the manner in which various contingencies are interdependent in their mutual moulding of the structure of local government.

CHAPTER 6

The Impacts of
Situational Contingencies

INTRODUCTION

In the previous chapter it was suggested that the organization of a local authority will be influenced by, and adapted to, a range of situational circumstances. These circumstances act as constraints because a local authority has to take account of, and react to, them. By law the local authority has to provide services of particular kinds for the population living in its area; it has to respond to the problems of its population; it has to take account of the resources available from that population and from other sources; it has to react to demands articulated from within that population and from other sources such as central government. In reacting, responding, and taking account of, a local authority will alter, change, and develop its organizational apparatus and its system of management.

To find out whether the ideas and propositions put forward in the last chapter are correct immediately raises the problem of operational recognition. Any idea or concept (such as 'problems' or 'resources') has to be 'translated' into one or more 'measures' so that it is possible to see whether that concept helps in understanding a given situation. For example, we may say that the larger the size of a local authority then the greater the extent of differentiation. How do we actually demonstrate that one local authority *is* of a larger size than another? The idea of size is an abstract concept which has to be put into an operational language such as the number of employees, the population to be served, the number of tasks being carried out. Conceptual and operational languages are

125

separate but related. If the conceptual statement that size is related to extent of differentiation is reformulated into the operational statement that the number of employees is related to the number of departments, the latter statement does not catch the full richness and all the possibilities of the conceptual statement. There is always a gap. An operational language is always less satisfying than the conceptual because of the need for operational precision, a consequence of which is a failure to capture nuances. The task of the researcher is to argue the relationship between his particular empirical operational measures and the conceptual problems that he has set himself to study. The first part of this chapter, therefore, outlines the operational measures used for the concepts of 'problems', 'resources', 'size', 'functional diversity' and 'accountability'. The task of the reader is to continuously question the relevance of the empirical measures to the conceptual language, while at the same time recognizing both the difficulties of, and necessities for, such measures. Readers who wish to examine the results of our enquiry, without considering the problem of operational measurement, should skip the next section and turn to p. 131.

THE OPERATIONAL MEASURES OF SITUATIONAL CONTINGENCIES

Environmental Characteristics

In the previous chapter it was proposed that the environment of a local authority contains two elements of interest here:

(1) the range and type of *problems* facing an authority,
(2) the supply and stability of *resources* available to it.

In seeking a measure of the range of environmental problems a useful starting point is to interpret problems as needs presented by the *age structure* of the population, the *social structure* of the population, and the *physical quality* of the area. Thus, it is reasonable to suppose that the existence of large numbers of people over the age of sixty-five, or of children of school age, or under five years of age, will put pressure upon the provision of various local authority services. They will create a need for schooling, social and recreational services, and so on. Thus, by calculating the percentage of the population under five, over sixty-five or of school age, the researcher obtains a partial measure of the problems facing an authority. The measure can be expanded to include problems arising from the social structure of the population. Working-class populations are liable to produce greater demands for services such as housing, social welfare, development planning and clearance. However, it is difficult to obtain information on social class for *local authority areas*. As a result proxy measures have to be used: that is, secondary measures known to have a strong relationship to social class. Two such measures will be used: the percentage of families receiving rent rebate, and the population density (the number of people per hectare).

A further aspect of local social structures which may present problems to a local authority is the presence of immigrants. A high number of immigrants may produce additional pressures for housing, a greater need for particular forms of enforcement activity, and problems of schooling and social welfare. Thus, our measure of range of problems includes the percentage of the population born outside the United Kingdom.

The physical quality of a local authority area can be approached in a number of ways. Physically a local authority is made up of roads, houses, schools, residential establishments, parks and open spaces, sports centres, etc. These all require maintenance, upkeep and sometimes demolition. For example, the housing department of a local authority is concerned with the problems of maintaining its council housing stock. Similarly, an environmental health department may put a great deal of organized effort into dealing with the improvement of houses. Because of the importance of the housing stock to all metropolitan and shire districts, our measures of the physical quality of the environment are centred on housing. Three measures of the quality of housing will be used, namely, the percentage of households in council houses, the percentage of households in privately owned houses, and the percentage of persons living more than one to a room. Our measure of the range of environmental problems, in other words, is based upon indicators of the age and social structure of the population, and the physical quality of the area. These are:

Age structure   % of population aged under 5
                 % of population aged over 65
                 % of population of school age

Social structure   % of population receiving rent rebate
                     % immigrant population
                     population density

Physical quality   % of population in council housing
                     % of persons living more than one to a room

The local authority has to respond to these problems taken together. Thus, the next step is to combine these separate indicators into a single measure. Each of the eight measures proposed has been divided at the mean and turned into a dichotomous variable and scored 2 for high on the problem and 1 for low. By adding the scores for each of the eight measures it is possible to obtain an indicator of *range* of problems faced. A local authority scoring 16 would have more than the average proportions of old people, children of school age, children under the age of five, a higher than average population density, many council houses, more immigrants, and so on. A local authority scoring 8 would have lower than average proportions. This scoring arrangement gets at the existence of many or few substantial environmental problems.

A further aspect of the problems facing a local authority concerns what in Chapter 5 is called the *types* of problems. A number of writers have attempted to classify towns in Britain (cf. Moser and Scott, 1961) using techniques for clustering indicators to produce types. We have used that development by Webber and Craig (1976) which covers the district level of local government. Their framework allows a distinction to be made between districts facing different classes of problems.

The second aspect of environment, the resources available, was described in the previous chapter in terms of absolute wealth, and the relative stability of resource supply. In seeking operational measures for these concepts attention will be restricted to financial resources: other resources, such as people and land, will be ignored. A useful measure of *wealth* is the volume of assets (rateable value) of the authority, especially in relation to the scale of population to be served. *Stability* of resources is measured using the figures provided by Jackman and Sellars (1977) for the metropolitan districts and shire counties, based upon the percentage change in rate support grant for each of these authorities between 1974/5 and 1977/8. We have no measure of resource instability for the shire districts. Thus, the operational measures of the resource environment are as follows:

Wealth: Rateable value per head
Stability: % change in RSG, 1974-8

Organizational Characteristics

In Chapter 5 it was suggested that a local authority has to respond to certain kinds of characteristics which are part of its own fabric. Although part of the local authority they can be conceptualized as influencing the authority's structural arrangements. Three characteristics were identified as important: size, task (functional diversity), and public accountability.

The idea of size is concerned with the magnitude of an authority's activities, that is, with the volume of tasks and people. Child (1973) has suggested that the crucial 'volume' for an organization is that of people, as 'it is people who are organized'. In other words, because it is people that have to be co-ordinated and controlled, that is, 'organized', then the appropriate form of organizational structure will reflect the number of people. An obvious operational measure, therefore, is the number of employees of a council. But there is a further and perhaps more important aspect of this idea within a local authority, namely, the number of elected representatives. Part of the organization and management of a local authority is devoted to the arena of *formal* activity among councillors — the committee. There is a continual tension between the size of a committee and the attitudes held by councillors that they should participate as widely as possible. The smaller the number of councillors, the more easily can the local authority reduce its committees without having to significantly reduce the degree of councillor participation and involvement. For this reason we use a second measure of size, the number of councillors.

Task, as indicated in the previous chapter, is an idea which, although central to much analysis of organizational structures, has been little used in the study of governmental organizations. Our approach, in order to deal with the distinctive nature of local authorities, is to emphasize the diversity of tasks performed. This underlines the differences between types of local authorities. The shire districts are the least diverse, having responsibility for housing and environmental health plus a limited role in recreation and planning. Metropolitan counties are a little more diverse, having responsibility for land-use planning, recreation, consumer protection, fire and police, and transportation. The shire counties are even more diverse, having responsibility for land-use planning, recreation, education, social services, highways, libraries and fire. Finally, the metropolitan districts and the outer London boroughs are the most diverse, combining many of the functions of the shire counties with most of the functions of the shire districts. In other words, the distinctions between local authority types can be used as a proxy measure of functional diversity by ranking them in the following way:

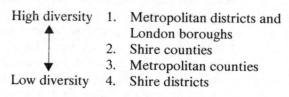

High diversity 1. Metropolitan districts and
               London boroughs
           2. Shire counties
           3. Metropolitan counties
Low diversity 4. Shire districts

This is an admittedly simple operational measure, taking little account of the complexity or diversity of tasks within a major function. Furthermore, it is debatable whether the metropolitan districts or the shire counties have the more diverse tasks. Nevertheless, it will suffice for present purposes to use this measure given the absence of a more sophisticated instrument.

A word of caution needs to be entered. In many ways, type of local authority is a mask for a whole range of differences between authorities. As well as indicating the diversity of tasks, types of authority differ significantly in their number of employees, their environmental problems and resource opportunities. Thus, any differences in organizational pattern cannot be clearly attributed to diversity of task; they may be due to these other differences. Thus, while we shall utilize the general notion of functional diversity as an aspect of technology the results presented below must be interpreted with care.

Public accountability has been defined to cover both party control and the extent of political organization. Our measure of party control, quite simply, is based upon which party holds a majority of seats on the council. There are several possibilities: Labour, Conservative, Liberal, Independents, Plaid Cymru. An authority without a party holding a majority of seats is classified as operating with no overall control. No attempt was made to measure the strength of party control (that is, the size of the majority in relation to other parties). Party control, as already emphasized, only deals with part of the impact of public accountability. *Who* controls is important but so, too, is *how* they exercise control. A party may have a majority of seats on the council but still allow the minority parties to take a major role in the running of the local authority. They may allow minority party members, for example, to be chairmen of certain committees. On the other hand, a majority party may provide all the chairmen, insist that all committees reflect the party balance of the council, hold caucus meetings regularly to establish policies, expect party members to vote at committee and council in line with party policy, and discipline members who do not do so. This difference in form of control is assessed using the index of political organization developed by Greenwood and Hinings (1976).

CONTINGENCIES AND STRUCTURE

The remaining sections of this chapter seek to explain why a local authority has a particular organizational system. The key word is *explain*: the focus of previous chapters has been descriptive. As a starting point it is worth recalling that the organizational patterns discussed in Chapter 4 were summations of three dimensions, namely, extent of differentiation, extent of integration, and style of integration (concentration). The purpose here is to show how contingencies operate to produce higher or lower amounts of differentiation and integration: in short, we have to test the hypotheses of Chapter 5. If the hypotheses are supported then it will, ipso facto, be possible to explain the differing patterns of organization.

For example, if one can show that (1) the larger the range of problems served by a local authority the greater the extent of differentiation and the more concentrated the style of integration, and (2) the greater the degree of political organization the greater the extent of integration, then it is possible to conclude that a highly political local authority serving a community with many problems will have a pattern E form of organization. Similarly, if the authority has a high measure of political organization but faces *few* environmental problems then it will have a pattern F structure (high differentiation, high integration and deconcentration). In other words, if one can determine the causes of the three organizational dimensions one can then make statements about the mix of environmental and organizational contingencies that will produce particular organizational patterns. It will also be possible to examine some rather more complex problems concerning the interrelationships of the causal factors and the possibility that a local authority may face conflicting constraints. However, the starting point must be to explain variations in the three organizational dimensions. In short, the hypotheses put forward in the previous chapter will be examined. These were:

1. The greater the range of substantial problems facing an authority the more differentiated and integrated will be its structure.

2. The greater the wealth available to a local authority, the more differentiated and less integrated will be its structure. It is also likely to have a deconcentrated style of integration.

3. An unstable supply of resources will result in lower differentiation, either higher or lower integration, and more or less concentration.

4. Larger local authorities will be more differentiated and integrated, and will have a more deconcentrated style of integration than smaller authorities.

5. The greater the functional diversity the greater the extents of differentiation and integration, and of a deconcentrated style.

6. The greater the degree of political organization the more likely it is that the local authority will adopt a concentrated style of integration.

7. Labour-controlled authorities will be more integrated and more differentiated than are Conservative-controlled authorities.

These hypotheses will be examined in turn, but not in the above sequence. Instead, hypothesis 5 will be taken first. This is because the operational measure of functional diversity is based upon a ranking of type of authority. Once that hypothesis has been examined we will consider the remaining hypotheses for each type of authority, thus removing the effect of local authority type.

Hypothesis 5: Functional Diversity

The suggestion is that the more tasks performed by a local authority
the more the authority's management structure will be differentiated, integrated and deconcentrated. A multiplicity of tasks will
create the need for greater numbers of committees and departments, which in turn will create the need for various co-ordinating
arrangements, of deconcentrated form, to handle the problem of
co-ordinating and controlling the growing volume of interactions
between them. How far this suggestion is empirically correct is
summarized in Table 6.1 which gives the mean scores by type of
authority.

TABLE 6.1   Relationship of Functional Diversity and Structural Form
Average Scores

High functional diversity	Differentiation	Integration	Concentration
metropolitan authorities	26.13	23.65	28.10
shire counties	27.27	23.71	29.73
metropolitan counties	17.00	25.00	29.00
shire districts	12.05	20.58	29.70
Low functional diversity			

Table 6.1 indicates that there is little support for the hypothesis as
formulated. That is, the differences by type of authority on the
extent and style of integration are largely insignificant. Thus, the
style of integration (concentration) is unaffected by functional
diversity: the average scores for each type of authority are similar.
The extent of integration is also unaffected by functional diversity,
with three types of authority operating with similar average scores,
despite variation in functional responsibilities. Only the shire
districts are different and even here the difference is not unduly
marked. There does seem to be support, however, for the view
that functional diversity affects the extent of differentiation. The
metropolitan authorities and the shire counties have much greater

extents of differentiation than either the metropolitan counties or the shire districts. If it is remembered that the operational measure (type of authority) is somewhat crude, then this marked difference between the two pairs of authorities, which quite clearly differ in their functional diversity, suggests that it would be reasonable to conclude that the hypothesized link between diversity and differentiation is supported. The lack of variation between the metropolitan authorities and the shire counties is probably a product of the insensitivity of the operational measure than of the hypothesis itself.

Hypotheses 1—4, 6, 7: The Shire Counties

The impact on the shire counties of contingencies other than functional diversity is provided as Table 6.2. It reveals that of the six hypotheses three are fully supported, two receive partial support, and that only one (hypothesis 6 is not supported). In the case of hypothesis 6 the data reveals the unanticipated result that political organization is associated with high rates of integration of *de*concentrated form.

The initial hypothesis (hypothesis 1) proposed that the range of environmental problems would be associated with the numbers of service *and* co-ordinating committees and departments. The more problems the more differentiation and integration. That hypothesis is fully confirmed. The response to a complex environment in the shire authorities is both to create more committees, sub-committees and departments, and to increase the number of formal mechanisms of co-ordination.

The range of environmental problems also affects the extent of concentration. The greater the range the more deconcentrated the style of integration. It would appear that one way of dealing with a range of environmental problems is to group services thought to have an affinity by introducing programme committees and directorates. Thus, certain counties have chosen to put together responsibility for planning and highways within the terms of reference of a single committee, or linked those functions through a joint sub-committee. This produces a more co-ordinated approach to problems and is consistent with a management style of pushing decisions down the organization, and away from

TABLE 6.2   *Constraints and Structure in the Shire Counties:*
Path Coefficients [a]

Contingencies	Organizational Structure		
	Extent of differentiation	Extent of integration	Extent of concentration (style)
A. Environmental			
(i) Problems			
range	0.62	0.54	−0.26
type			
(ii) Resources			
wealth		−0.24	
stability	−0.22		
B. Organizational			
(i) Size			
councillors			
employees	0.36	0.40	−0.21
(ii) Accountability			
political organization		0.39	−0.26
party control	0.40	0.23	
N = 44 *R²*	0.36	0.48	0.09

[a] Path coefficients are standardized partial regression coefficients. As such they show the effect of, for example, range of problems or extent of differentiation, holding other contingencies constant. All the path coefficients are more than twice their standard error — the R^2 is a multiple regression showing the percentage of variation explained in the dependent variable (e.g. extent of differentiation) by all the contingencies entered into the regression.

centrally based and concentrated co-ordinating machinery. Such an approach appears to be the response of those shire counties with an extensive array of environmental problems.

Hypotheses 2 and 3 are concerned with the availability and stability of resources. These environmental contingencies do not appear as important as environmental problems. Hypothesis 2 proposed that greater wealth would encourage greater differentiation and less integration. In fact, the results show an absence of effect upon differentiation: the anticipated connection with integration, on the other hand, is confirmed.

Those counties with the lowest supply of resources have the most integration, thus confirming the argument that decisions expressing clear priority between competing service areas are essential when there is a limited supply of resources. In order to establish such priorities the shire counties find it convenient to set up budget sub-committees, interdepartmental policy analysis groups, panels of members, and similar arrangements to carry out analysis and prepare the necessary information. The *stability* of resources, on the other hand, is (as expected) associated with the extent of differentiation but not at all (contrary to expectations) with the extent or style of integration.

Hypothesis 4, which states that larger local authorities will be more differentiated, integrated, and deconcentrated, is fully supported. The effects of accountability, on the other hand, are not entirely as expected. Party control *is* related to differentiation and integration as set out in hypothesis 7, i.e. Labour authorities are more differentiated and more integrated. But political organization does not operate as anticipated in hypothesis 6. Political organization does, however, affect the extent and style of integration. It was expected that a higher rate of political organization would create a more concentrated style of integration: in fact, the more organized the political parties, the more deconcentrated the style of integration throughout the authority as a whole. Why this should be the case is not clear. One possibility is that the extent of political organization in the shire counties has increased rapidly in recent years whereas the basic principles of the management structure are consistent with the political practices of the years preceding the 1974 Reorganization. There may be an institutional delay in responding to changed political circumstances. If this is the case, we would expect the shire authorities to become more concentrated as the pressures of political organization are felt.

The second effect of political organization was also unanticipated, although it is more easily understood. The original hypothesis argued that organized political parties would attempt to control the policies and decisions produced by the service committees and departments. That hypothesis is consistent with material collected through interviews with councillors of the sample of 27 local authorities. It was clear from those interviews that organized political parties are associated with developed political programmes and a clear desire to impress those programmes upon committee decisions *in an integrated manner*. The finding in Table 6.2 confirms this impression — that highly organized political parties work through higher extents of structural integration in order to co-ordinate decisions and policies.

There are, in other words, a number of contingencies each having identifiable effects upon the structures of local authorities. In particular it has been found that five contingencies — range of environmental problems, resource instability, wealth, organizational scale, public accountability — help determine the structures of the shire counties. The next step is to relate these findings to the eight organizational patterns previously identified. Let us be clear about the purpose of this step. Our argument has been that local authorities operate with different organizational forms, an argument demonstrated by identification of eight organizational patterns. We have also argued that these organizational differences are caused by situational conditions to which the local authority has to adapt. This claim has been supported already by studying the separate relationships of several contingencies to three aspects of structure. But the pattern of a local authority's organization is a response to a mixture of situational contingencies and it is our aim to illustrate how the blend of environmental and organizational contingencies produces various organizational patterns. In particular we shall examine the combination of circumstances producing patterns B (high integration, low differentiation, low concentration), E (High integration, high differentiation, high concentration) and G (low integration, high differentiation, high concentration). These represent the more common patterns of the shire counties.

Shire counties with pattern B structures are notable for the following environmental and organizational characteristics:

They face a wide range of environmental problems.
They have a limited availability of resources (i.e. low wealth).
They employ small numbers of employees and have small councils.
They are highly organized politically.

In other words, it is the small local authority with a complex environment but few resources which finds it convenient to operate with pattern B structures. Thus, the limited availability of resources makes the authority use a wide range of integrative arrangements (to avoid inefficiences and duplication) and the range of problems produces a deconcentrated style of integration. So, an *environment* characterized by many problems but limited resources is 'managed' by using many co-ordinating devices of deconcentrated form. The *organizational* characteristics of these authorities work in the same direction. Thus, the high degree of political organization produces a high measure of structural integration. In order to impose political priorities the majority party creates central co-ordinating arrangements. That is, these authorities emphasize the use of integrative structures partly in response to the environmental characteristics of limited resources, *and* partly in response to the demands of the organized political parties. Finally, the extent of differentiation is the result of the size of the authority. These authorities tend to be smaller than other shire counties, both in terms of employees and numbers of councillors. As a result there is less need for many departments and committees.

Pattern E local authorities are rather different in the environmental and organizational characteristics faced. They have the following characteristics:

a small range of environmental problems,
a limited availability of resources,
large numbers of employees and councillors,
a high measure of political organization.

In other words, these are the large, highly political authorities facing a rather less complex environment than those of pattern B. Pattern E authorities have limited resources but also have fewer environmental problems. Thus, *the environment* is managed through use of many integrative devices of a concentrated form. The lack of resources makes assessment of priorities a critical responsibility (hence the emphasis upon integrative machinery) but the limited scale of the problems to be handled makes it possible to determine priorities in a concentrated manner. Because there are few environmental problems the volume of decisions involved can be handled at a central, concentrated point: there is less need for deconcentrated structures. The *organizational characteristics* affect the extent of integration and differentiation. Again, the effect of political organization is consistent with the kind of environment faced. That is, political organization reinforces the environmental impulse for greater integration. This is the same arrangement observed for pattern B. But, the larger size of pattern E authorities produces an organizational structure characterized by many committees and departments, that is, a high rate of differentiation. The volume of activities and interactions is sufficient to warrant a larger number of committees, sub-committees and departments than is found under pattern B.

Pattern G authorities are different again. These authorities share with pattern E the situation of large scale and few environmental problems, but their considerable supply of resources and the lack of an organized political structure means that there is little pressure for the development of management systems which integrate the local authority as an entity. In short, pattern G local authorities are large, non-political, relatively wealthy, and face a limited range of environmental problems. To meet these environmental and organizational characteristics authorities operate through a management structure of high differentiation coupled with low and deconcentrated integration.

The above analysis leads to an emphasis on the 'situation-specific' nature of each shire county in an effort to understand why it has a particular management structure. The framework adopted has identified the generalized features likely to be important in understanding how such structures originate: these features are the range of environmental problems, the size of operation, attempts at political control, resource availability and resource stability. These appear to be the crucial variables shaping the structures of the shire counties. We have gone beyond this and suggested how a particular clustering of these contingencies produce a particular structure pattern. The following section performs the same analysis for the metropolitan authorities.

Hypotheses 1—4, 6, 7: The Metropolitan Authorities

For present purposes the metropolitan districts and the London boroughs are grouped together because they represent the majority of *urban* local government in this country. With the exception of the inner London boroughs, which do not carry out the education function, they have a very similar range of services. Table 6.3 indicates how these authorities adapt their organizational structures to the environmental and organizational constraints within which they have to operate.

TABLE 6.3   *Constraints and Structure in Metropolitan Authorities: Path Coefficients [a]*

| | Organizational structure | | |
| | | | |
Contingencies	Extent of differentiation	Extent of integration	Extent of concentration (style)
A. Environmental			
(i) Problems			
range	0.46	0.27	−0.32
type			
(ii) Resources			
wealth		0.21	
stability			
B. Organizational			
(i) Size			
councillors	0.26		−0.27
employees	0.64	−0.34	0.36
(ii) Accountability			
political organization		0.39	
party control	0.57		
$N = 59$ R^2	0.51	0.20	0.12

[a]   See footnote to Table 6.2.

The range of problems that a metropolitan authority faces are clearly related to the extents of differentiation and integration: the greater the range of problems, the greater will be the extent of differentiation. This is as anticipated in hypothesis 1. The volume of activity generated by the range of problems means that specialist departments and units are warranted and established. The range of problems also affects the extent of integration. As a result of their need to manage complex environments the metropolitan authorities set up management structures emphasizing an integrated response. That is, a complex range of environmental problems generates a volume of activity warranting a high rate of differentiation: it also produces the problem of interactions between policies, promoting the need for co-ordinative machinery. Hypothesis 1 is thus fully supported. Furthermore, there is an unanticipated result. Authorities facing a wide range of social, economic and physical problems will adopt a deconcentrated mode of operation. This finding is the same as that observed in the shire counties, and the same explanation applies here.

The hypothesis on wealth (hypothesis 2) is not supported either in terms of differentiation or deconcentration. The same hypothesis, moreover, is turned round by the results for integration. It was expected that wealthier authorities would be characterized by a lower emphasis on integrative structures. In fact, the wealthier metropolitan authorities are *more* integrated which is contrary to the results for the shire counties. We are unable to explain why this should be the case.

The effects of organizational size (hypothesis 4) are only partly as expected: Table 6.3 indicates that the larger the size of the metropolitan authority the more it will establish committees, sub-committees and departments (that is, increase the rate of differentiation). Both the number of councillors, as well as the sheer number of employees, demonstrates this impact. It seems that the volume of activity engendered, and the number of relationships to be handled, caused by increases in numbers of employees and councillors forces the metropolitan organization to divide its functions and tasks. This observation was expected. It was not expected, however, that size (indicated by number of employees) would produce *less* integration. This result is somewhat puzzling. As indicated in an earlier chapter the effects of size upon organizational structures have been extensively documented and provided consistent results. The findings in Table 6.3 are a rare instance of size producing a low extent of integration. There is nothing in our available data to suggest reasons for this occurrence. There is a further effect of size which is equally surprising, namely the association of numbers of employees with a concentrated style of integration. The larger the administration of an authority the more concentrated the style of integration. We can offer no explanation for this association.

The remaining effect of size is more amenable to theoretical suggestion. It appears that the larger the number of members on the council the more likely that the authority will operate through a deconcentrated style of integration. It is interesting to speculate on why this should be the case. As with central government more and more is heard in local government about the 'problem' of the backbencher. The division between the central leaders of local political parties and the rank-and-file backbenchers has become more apparent in recent years. The increase in political organiza-tion referred to earlier has served to mark and accentuate the relative status of leader and follower. In response to this, authorities are beginning to look for ways of bringing the ordinary member into the operation of the local authority. Working parties, panels of members, officer-member groups are devices being explored to involve the backbench councillor. These vehicles complement the committee system, acting as forums where wide-ranging discussions can take place. The net effect is that larger metropolitan authorities are consciously examining means of involving all members through *de*concentrated structural arrangements.

Hypothesis 6 on political organization is not confirmed. There is no evidence that a high degree of political organization leads to a concentrated style of integration. But, the finding of the shire counties is repeated in that political organization leads to more structural integration. In the metropolitan districts a dominant majority party seeks to implement its will through policy working parties and committees, performance review panels, and an assortment of resources sub-groups. These devices enable the party to enmesh itself in a wide range of decision areas, thus facilitating political control. The fact that this pattern is found in both the shire counties and the metropolitan authorities is significant, suggesting a strong association of political organization with the extent of structural integration irrespective of type of authority or party complexion.

In 1977, thirty-two of the sample of metropolitan authorities and London boroughs were Labour-controlled, twenty-three were Conservative, there was one Liberal authority, and three others lacked any party with an overall majority. A comparison of their structures indicates that Labour-controlled authorities are much more likely to be highly differentiated than are Conservative-controlled authorities, as anticipated in hypothesis 7. This is consistent with the arguments of the Maud Committee. That Committee suggested that Labour-controlled administrations are likely to pay more attention to detail, resulting in a requirement for larger numbers of committees and sub-committees to manage the transaction of detailed business. This is confirmed by the results for metropolitan authorities. Labour authorities in the metropolitan areas, however, are *not* likely to make use of additional formal integrative machinery. Unlike Labour authorities in the shire counties they do not have more policy and resource committees, or sub-committees, supported by co-ordinating arrangements at officer levels. This is contrary to the expectation in hypothesis 7.

There are, in summary, a considerable number of contingencies operating upon the structures of metropolitan authorities. The range of environmental problems faced, the availability of resources, the scale of the authority, the degree of political organization and the complexion of party control work to shape the structures of the metropolitan districts and the London boroughs. An important question, therefore, is how these organizational and environmental contingencies combine in their effects. We shall consider the circumstances that produce the more commonly found arrangements for the metropolitan authorities, namely, organizational patterns D, A and F.

Metropolitan authorities with a pattern D structure operate with relatively few committees and departments (low differentiation), few co-ordinating committees and departments (low integration) and practise a deconcentrated system of involvement and accountability. There is little difficulty in explaining the first two of these structural features. They occur at least partly because these authorities are set within an environment characterized by

  low wealth, and

  a small range of environmental problems.

These features taken together produce low differentiation and low integration. Because these authorities face a limited array of environmental problems they do not need large numbers of committees and departments. Furthermore, the rather low availability of resources prevents the adoption of complicated integrative machinery. In short, the environment pushes these authorities towards low differentiation and low integration.

Such authorities also have two organizational characteristics consistent with a pattern D form of organization. Thus, they tend to be controlled by the Conservative Party (a feature which encourages low differentiation) and exhibit low political organization (which discourages the development of integrative machinery). In other words, the distinctive environmental and organizational characteristics of these authorities combine to work in the same direction to produce a low extent of differentiation, and a low extent of integration.

But what of the style of integration? Why do these authorities operate with a deconcentrated style of operation? These questions are important because the *environmental* characteristics identified above would lead us to expect a concentrated style of integration. According to Table 6.3 local authorities coping with few environmental problems will adopt a concentrated style. But this is clearly not the case for certain metropolitan authorities. Some metropolitan authorities have constructed a *de*concentrated set of arrangements, despite facing few environmental problems. The answer to this apparent conundrum lies in the number of councillors. Table 6.3 indicates that the larger local authorities (those with larger numbers of councillors) tend to operate through a deconcentrated pattern of integration. It is this association which is causing pattern D authorities to have deconcentrated arrangements *despite* the low complexity of the environment. Pattern D authorities have responded to a characteristic of their organization and in doing so ignored pressures from the environment. Faced with contradictory impulses these local authorities have the opportunity of responding to one of two important contingencies, but not both. They have chosen to respond to the exigencies of scale but not to the exigencies of environmental complexity. We shall encounter this dilemma again and will comment upon it further at that point.

Pattern A local authorities have a similarly complicated array of contingencies. They are characterized by

a small range of environmental problems,
a substantial pool of available resources (high wealth),
small scale (small numbers of employees and councillors),
a high degree of political organization,
a Conservative-controlled council.

In some respects these environmental and organizational contingencies are not contradictory. They produce the same effects upon the local authority. Thus the small range of environmental problems is effectively handled through low differentiation and a concentrated style of integration. The authority also has a small number of councillors and employees, a characteristic similarly associated with low differentiation. A small authority does not have the volume of activity to warrant many committees, sub-committees and departments. In other words, pattern A authorities have environmental (range of problems) and organizational (size) characteristics which push in the same direction. In other respects, however, pattern A authorities have to cope with inconsistent contingencies, especially in the design of integrative structures. On the one hand, the low range of environmental problems presses for few co-ordinating arrangements, and of a concentrated form. The fact that these authorities are usually controlled by the Conservative Party, and have a low rate of political organization, also presses towards lower use of integrative structures. But the size of the authority, according to Table 6.3 works in the reverse direction, pressing for more integration and a deconcentrated style.

All of this is becoming increasingly complicated, and in one sense it is unimportant to labour the details of the impact of multiple contingencies upon pattern A structures. The important point is that to understand why any authority has a particular structural form it is necessary to recognize that the present structure is a response to *possibly inconsistent contingencies.* Pattern A metropolitan authorities have clearly responded to the exigencies of certain contingencies and not others. These authorities *cannot* meet the pressures of all contingencies acting upon them. As a result they may become increasingly unstable as they seek to accommodate to the stresses and strains associated with the lack of structural association with particular contingencies.

Pattern F metropolitan authorities are much simpler. Their environments are characterized by a wide range of substantial problems, and a limited availability of resources. Organizationally they are characterized by high political organization and are likely to be Labour-controlled. These contingencies produce a high measure of differentiation, of integration and of deconcentration. In short, there is a consistency between the pressures of the environment and those of the organization.

One tentative idea to be put forward here is that metropolitan authorities may tend to be rather more organizationally unstable than the shire counties. We have identified two of the three most important organizational patterns within the metropolitan areas as the products of inconsistent contingencies. These authorities are pushed and pulled in different directions by the contingencies acting upon them, unlike the counties where the relationships between constraints and organizational pattern tend not to exhibit such conflicting pressures. Perhaps this underlines that urban areas face more complex sets of contingencies than do other areas and suggests that the organizational and managerial response to such problems is by no means clear-cut and may exhibit some of the complexity and instability of the environment they face.

Hypotheses 1—4, 6, 7: The Shire Districts

In discussing the shire districts it is necessary to emphasize the considerable differences in environmental and organizational characteristics that exist between these local authorities. Not only are they very different from the shire counties and the metropolitan authorities in their relative scale and function, but they vary amongst themselves to a much greater extent than do the counties or metropolitan districts. At one end of the spectrum is Radnor District Council with 23,000 inhabitants; at the other end is Bristol D.C., serving a population greater than 400,000. There are also differences in environment and politics. It is in the districts that the last 'stronghold' of the non-partisan council is found (Grant, 1978). Very often, even those districts that appear to be politically organized are very different from the metropolitan districts: the party political label can mean very little. Again, there are districts set within environments of an entirely urban form contrasting with others of more rural form. There are districts covering very large geographical areas (Alnwick covers 108,000 hectares) and those which are highly constricted (Gosport has only 2,518 hectares).

The heterogeneity of the shire district councils offers the possibility of rather better and stronger correlations with structure. If the management structure of a local authority *is* a response to its environmental and organizational situation then the wider the variation in such situations the better the test of the hypotheses. The smaller variation among the shire counties, and among the metropolitan districts and London boroughs, raises the possibility that a low level of correlations may be a result of the numbers of authorities within the sample itself, rather than attributable to a 'failure' of the local authority to adapt to its situation. Both the wider differences in situation of shire districts and their greater number provide the opportunity for a stronger test of our ideas. We should recognize, however, that only five of the hypotheses are relevant to the shire districts. Hypothesis 3, linking the stability of resource supply to structure, is not applicable because of the particular operational measure used.

According to Table 6.4 the shire district is particularly responsive to the range and type of problems within its environment. It is not responsive to problems of resource availability. That is, the range and type of problems impact upon structure, but the availability of resources (absolute wealth) does not. Hypothesis 2, in other words, is not supported. Hypothesis 1, however, is fully supported: the more problems a local authority faces the more differentiated and integrated will be its structure. The greater the range of problems faced by a shire district the greater are the pressures for a management structure which differentiates the authority's decision-making response to that complex environment. And, in the process of coping with such environmental pressures the local authority has to produce a co-ordinated response; hence its high level of integration. It was not expected that the range of environmental problems would produce a deconcentrated style of integration. The shire districts, however, do provide such an association in the same way that it was found for the metropolitan districts and the shire counties. The same explanation offered above is equally relevant here.

There is another hypothesis fully supported by the material in Table 6.4, namely, that linking the size of the authority with the

TABLE 6.4   *Constraints and Structure in Shire Districts:*
Path Coefficients [a]

Contingencies	Organizational structure		
	Extent of differentiation	Extent of integration	Extent of concentration (style)
A. Environmental			
(i) Problems			
range	0.38	0.12	−0.12
type	0.19		
(ii) Resources			
wealth			
stability			
B. Organizational			
(i) Size			
councillors	0.36	0.40	
employees	0.40	0.27	
(ii) Accountability			
political organization	0.17	0.19	
party control	0.52		
N = 302 R^2	0.30	0.22	0.05

[a] See footnote to Table 6.2.

extent of differentiation and integration. The greater the number of employees and of councillors, the more likely it is that the shire districts will increase its use of departments, service committees and sub-committees. From this development arise the problems of control, co-ordination and communication dealt with by the creation of additional numbers of co-ordinating committees and officer structures. That is, the larger shire districts operate with greater measures of both differentiation and integration.

The extent of political organization (hypothesis 6) is clearly linked with particular structures but not in ways set out within the original hypothesis. The original formulation suggested that greater political organization would lead to a concentrated style of integration. This is not the case in the shire districts. But political organization is strongly connected to differentiation and integration, both increasing as the local authority becomes politically organized. One of these effects has already been noted above in the discussion both on the shire counties and the metropolitan authorities. Political organization, it was noted, prompts the creation of various co-ordinating structures as the majority party seeks to exercise its political will. Political organization produces a high level of integration in all authorities, irrespective of type. The other finding — that political organization increases the extent of differentiation — is found only in the shire districts. Why this should be the case is not immediately apparent from the data at our disposal.

The effects of party political control, it was hypothesized, would touch the extents of differentiation and of integration. In particular, Labour-controlled authorities would be more differentiated and integrated than Conservative authorities. In fact, many of the shire districts are of 'Independent' control, and it is interesting that it is these authorities that are influenced. In particular, districts controlled by Independents are significantly less differentiated than either the Labour- or Conservative-controlled districts. In contrast, there is little or no difference between authorities controlled by the Labour or Conservative parties, thus refuting hypothesis 7 as set out. Hypothesis 7 was also incorrect in proposing a link between party control and extent of integration. Extent of integration is unaffected by the complexion of the controlling party.

Before turning to discussion of organizational patterns it is worth noting the absence of any strong associations between environmental and organizational contingencies and the *style* of integration. All that exists is the suggestion that the range of environmental problems increases the likelihood of a deconcentrated style of operation.

What, then, do these relationships mean for the differences in patterns of organization that have been found between shire districts? As with the previous discussions we shall limit ourselves to examining those organizational patterns containing the larger numbers of authorities. These are patterns C, A, D and F. It is interesting to note that the last three of these are also the most common patterns for metropolitan authorities. C is the only new organizational pattern.

A pattern C shire district has a straightforward contextual profile; all of the environmental and organizational constraints are acting with a similar effect. These authorities have the following characteristics:

a low range of environmental problems,
low political organization,
a small number of employees and councillors,
a tendency for Independents to be the largest political group.

Taken together these characteristics provide the typical profile of the rural district to be found in counties such as Cumbria, Cornwall and Northumberland, as well as in Powys and Dyfed. Compared with other local authorities there is less pressure, both in terms of problems faced and the volume of activity. Thus, there is no great need for large numbers of committees, departments and specialists. The extent of necessary differentiation, in short, is low. Furthermore, the low range of problems and the relatively small scale of the organization make structural integration less difficult: relationships between services do not figure as a serious problem and it is possible to operate with a low emphasis on structural co-ordination. The style of integration appropriate to these conditions, moreover, is one of structural concentration.

There is a second organizational pattern — pattern F — which also exhibits contextual 'consistency'. It is a pattern found in large local authorities facing a wide range of environmental problems, and operating with a high degree of political organization. These authorities will be controlled by either the Labour or Conservative Party. Because of the range of environmental problems, coupled with the volume of activity generated from the large size of the authority there will be a relatively large number of committees and departments; but, because of the complex nature of the environment (the large range of problems), it is also necessary for the local authority to set up integrative devices in order to obtain a sensitive and co-ordinated policy response. Similarly, the complexity of the environment will produce pressures for a deconcentrated style of integration. The extent of political organization will reinforce the tendency towards high differentiation and integration. These local authorities are the large urban shire districts such as Nottingham, Derby and Southampton.

Of the remaining organizational patterns A is more complicated and for that reason rather interesting. We know that shire districts with pattern A structures are low on differentiation, high on integration, and are concentrated in style. They have these characteristics because of their peculiar blend of situational characteristics. These authorities face a small range of environmental problems and as a consequence face pressures to keep to a minimum the numbers of service and co-ordinating committees and departments. There is no need (in environmental terms) for large numbers of differentiated structural parts, or for an extensive apparatus for co-ordination. In response to environmental pressures, in other words, the shire districts within this category should operate with low differentiation, low integration and high concentration. However, these districts also have a number of characteristics working in a contradictory direction:

They have a large number of councillors.
They have a large number of employees.

These circumstances produce pressures for more differentiation and more integration. The shire district, in short, will be able to set up a deconcentrated style of integration in response to its environmental circumstances because there are no other contingencies working against such a development. But, the development of greater differentiation and integration (in response to the exigencies of organizational size) would be directly contradictory to the exigencies of the environment. These authorities, as with some of the metropolitan districts, have to cope with a set of *environmental* contingencies whose impulse is one direction (low differentiation and low integration) and a set of *organizational* contingencies working in the reverse direction (high differentiation and high integration). Inevitably, these authorities will experience the internal stresses consequent upon an inability to accommodate contradictory impulses arising from their situational conditions. They may find it convenient to change their structures as the various stresses become uncomfortable: having done so, other stresses will arise, thus producing an unstable organizational form.

Districts with pattern D structures are rather less complicated. These authorities operate with low differentiation and low integration and are deconcentrated. They face a small range of environmental problems, have a tendency towards 'Independent' control, and are rather low in terms of political organization. All of these contingencies work in the same direction. The environmental *and* organizational conditions press for low extents of committee and departmental differentiation and integration. Furthermore, the limited range of environmental problems is appropriately handled through a concentrated style of integration. Pattern D authorities have little difficulty accommodating to their prevalent environmental and organizational conditions.

CONCLUSIONS

In this chapter our purpose has been to explore how far differences observed in the structural arrangements of local authorities are the product of different environmental and organizational characteristics. In Chapter 5 it was argued that there is a variety of situational circumstances to which a local authority must respond. This means that a purely legal description of what the authority does, and of how it performs its legal responsibilities, is inadequate. To understand how a local authority is organized the mix and incidence of important contingencies have to be considered. In this chapter we have examined how far these arguments are empirically valid, and a number of conclusions may be drawn.

As a starting point the results presented above have indicated that local authority management structures are related to their environmental and organizational circumstances. All authorities, for example, irrespective of the range of functions performed, are affected by:

the range of environmental problems,
the scale of the organization (number of employees),

the extent of political organization,
party control.

These contingencies need not, however, produce the same structural effect in all types of authorities. In the case of environmental complexity the effect *is* the same for all authorities. The greater the range of problems the more differentiated, the more integrated and the more deconcentrated will be the authority. We can make that observation of *any* local authority. But the effects of organizational size, and of political organization, are less straightforward. For example, the larger shire counties tend to be more differentiated, more integrated, and *less* concentrated in style than the smaller counties. In contast, the larger metropolitan authorities (as measured by numbers of employees) tend to be more differentiated, *less* integrated, and *more* concentrated in style. The shire districts differ again in that the style of integration (concentration) is untouched by organizational size. We could make similar observations concerning the effects of political organization and of party control. Indeed, a full summary of the results of this chapter is provided in the next chapter. The important point to note here is that the metropolitan and shire districts, and the shire counties, are all affected in some way by the variety of environmental problems, the scale of the organization, the measure of political organization, and the complexion of party control.

The remaining contingencies — the availability and stability of resources — have a more limited relevance. Metropolitan districts and the shire counties are affected by the availability of resources, whereas the shire districts are not. The crucial part of the environment for the shire districts is the range of problems to be managed: the management structure is designed to meet the pattern of needs and does not reflect the availability of resources. The shire counties and metropolitan authorities are rather more affected by environmental problems and resources, although even in these cases the range of problems is both more extensive and significant in its impact.

These differences between types of authorities in the relative importance of particular contingencies, and in the nature of their effects, will not be explored here. A fuller exposition is contained in the concluding chapter. It is more important to stress that this chapter has demonstrated the manner in which authorities facing different situational contingencies have developed different management structures. The effects of situational circumstances have been explored in two ways. At the beginning of the chapter each contingency was considered in turn and its structural consequences discussed. That approach provided a clear understanding of the impact of particular contingencies. Later, we discussed how a local authority responds to a blend of contingencies. We demonstrated how a combination of environmental and organizational factors produce particular patterns of organizational design. Thus, it was noted that shire districts facing a wide range of environmental problems, and whose organizational characteristics include a high measure of political organization, and large scale, will be highly differentiated, highly integrated, and have a deconcentrated style of integration. Combining the effects of situational contingencies made it possible to explain the broad organizational patterns appropriate to individual authorities.

Discussion of how contingencies act in combination is important for at least two reasons. First, as indicated earlier, local authorities themselves respond to contingencies in terms of organizational patterns. At times, authorities may tinker with limited parts of their structure, but the broad features of the organization are more likely to be established in coherent rather than separate fashion. It is sensible, therefore, that we should discuss structures as patterned responses, rather than as a number of separate piecemeal reforms. Secondly, and perhaps more interestingly, it is by identifying patterns and relating them to environmental and organizational conditions that we have observed the difficulties of responding to contradictory contingencies. Some authorities face contingencies whose structural effects are in conflict, making it impossible to adjust to both at the same time. To meet one contingency is to flout another. The theoretical consequences of this will be explored in more detail in the next chapter where we shall consider the idea of organizational choice. But it is worth noting that the existence of contradictory impulses from situational contingencies may well be a factor producing organizational instability. By identifying the existence of contradictory contingencies we have introduced a possible explanation of organization *change*. In the next chapter we shall explore this notion further. In particular, we shall review how far the data of this and the previous chapters have met the purposes established at the outset of the analysis. How far have we provided explanations of organizational variations and change?

CHAPTER 7

Conclusions

Chapter 1 set two tasks for the analysis to follow: *first*, to demonstrate how far local authorities differed in their structural arrangements; and *second*, to explain *why* local authorities have different structures and why they change. In particular, it was argued that structural differences are in part the product of situational conditions. Local authorities are set within different environments and have different organizational characteristics: these environments and organizational characteristics produce differences in structure and can offer some explanation for persistent structural reorganization. Hence, this volume has sought to map out, and explain, the complexity and instability of local authority organizational structures. How far has it succeeded?

The description of local authority structures was based upon four organizational dimensions: the extent and criteria of differentiation, and the extent and style of integration. These dimensions were selected because they represent the fundamental and complementary processes underlying questions of organizational design. The contemporary importance of these dimensions was indicated in Chapter 2 which reviewed the recent history of organizational reform within local government in England and Wales. In Chapter 2 each dimension was taken in turn and the degrees of variation between local authorities were plotted. On three dimensions significant differences were found. The criteria of differentiation demonstrated rather less variation: local authorities as a whole employ the same criteria, using a combination of service and programme committees. Despite such lack of variation on this single structural dimension, a number of interesting experiments were noted, especially with area forms of committee and departmental management. Taken as a whole, however, local authorities were found to vary in their extents of differentiation and integration and their style of integration, but not in their use of alternative criteria of differentiation. At the end of Chapter 3 it was possible to conclude that the initial assumption of the book, namely, that variation exists, was justified. That conclusion was reinforced in Chapter 4 when the analysis turned to *patterns* of organization. By combining three of the four organizational dimensions eight organizational patterns were produced. Local authorities were located within each pattern and the relative popularity of each was demonstrated. In this way we were able to represent the total responses of local authorities to the structural issues of how many committees and departments are appropriate, to what extent they should be integrated by various formal co-ordinative arrangements, and what should be the style of that integrative machinery. Having done so, an attempt was made to predict the kinds of problems that might be associated with each organizational pattern. For example, it was suggested that management teams within patterns A and B would experience the dilemma of collective responsibility to the policy committee alongside the individual responsibility of a service chief officer to a committee chairman. It was also pointed out that pattern A raised in acute form the supplanting of the traditional relationship linking officers to the council by a model of accountability more akin to that operating within the civil service. These and other suggestions to do with operational difficulties were largely drawn from work undertaken in 1974-8 on a sample of 27 local authorities, the results of which are reported more fully elsewhere (Hinings *et al.*, 1980).

It was always envisaged that the identification of inter-authority variation would be a comparatively easy stage of analysis. Much more difficult would be to provide explanation. One approach towards explanation would be to focus upon the processes of *choice* within an organization, tracing the interactions of interested and influential parties over certain key decisions. This approach would see organizational form and organizational change as the product of a strategic choice made by the influential or dominant coalition of interested parties. More will be made of this approach in a moment. The alternative approach, adopted in Chapters 5 and 6, focuses upon the *constraints* upon the choices available to decision makers. Constraints arise from the existence of important contingencies to which the local authority has to respond, and which it cannot change in the short term. These contingencies are 'givens' and circumscribe the actions and opportunities of decision makers seeking to make choices about structural design.

Two groups of contingencies were identified as of possible importance to local government. There are those emanating from the environment, concerned with the range of problems with which the authority has to cope, and the volume and stability of available resources. On the other hand, there are characteristics of the local authority itself, such as the size of the organization, the diversity of its tasks, the political complexion of the council, and the incidence of political organization. How far these contingencies *do* act as constraints over the choice of structure, and therefore help to explain differences in local authority practices, was explored in Chapter 6. Given the theoretical importance of that analysis it is worth rehearsing the main findings, of which a summary is provided in Table 7.1.

ENVIRONMENTAL CHARACTERISTICS

The range of environmental problems facing an authority tends to affect its structural arrangements irrespective of type of authority. That is, both counties and districts in the metropolitan and shire areas are affected by the number of substantive environmental problems with which they have to cope. The specific nature of that effect, moreover, is common to each type of authority. A wider range of problems produces greater differentiation, more integration, and a deconcentrated style of integration. These findings were understandable. The volume and complexity of business involved in handling a complex of environmental problems is a natural cause of structural differentiation. Indeed, differentiation is justified throughout the literature of organizational theory as the vehicle for securing a specialized response to sets of specialized demands. It is similarly not difficult to understand why a range of environmental problems should produce a high measure of integrative machinery *and* a deconcentrated style of integration.

TABLE 7.1 *The Effect of Environmental and Organizational Characteristics upon Local Authority Structures:*
A Summary[a]

Contingencies	Shire districts			Shire counties			Metropolitan authorities		
	Different-iation	Integ-ration	Style of Integration	Different-iation	Integ-ration	Style of Integration	Different-iation	Integ-ration	Style of Integration
Environment									
Problems	Yes	Yes	Yes	Yes	Yes	Yes	Yes	Yes	Yes
Resources	No	No	No	Yes	Yes	No	No	Yes	No
Organization									
Size	Yes	Yes	No	Yes	Yes	Yes	Yes	Yes	Yes
Political organization	Yes	Yes	No	No	Yes	Yes	No	Yes	No
Party control	Yes	No	No	Yes	Yes	No	Yes	No	No

[a] The Yes/No indicates whether the contingency affects the particular aspect of structure.

Again, it is the complexity and volume of business required of the authority in its attempts to manage the complex environment that is the principal variable. Because of the large amount of business, and the sheer intellectual complexity of it, any centralized attempt to co-ordinate policies and decisions would result in lengthy delays, little integration, or both. A deconcentrated style of integration is the only feasible approach under conditions where there are many problems with many interactions.

Rather different conclusions must be drawn from the effects of the second environmental characteristic — the availability and stability of resources. The availability of resources has (a) no impact upon the shire districts, (b) increases the extent of structural integration in metropolitan authorities, and (c) decreases the extent of integration in the shire counties. That is, the wealthier metropolitan authorities are prompted to use more integrative arrangements whereas the wealthier counties are prompted to use less. Possibly this apparent contradiction in effect may be the result of the different mixes and intensities of problems faced by shire and metropolitan authorities. The latter, more conscious of the critical overlay of environmental problems packed together in a metropolitan setting, may be more sensitive to the claimed advantages of a more integrated approach. The shire counties, on the other hand, are, on the whole, less confronted with acute interactions of environmental problems. The shire counties have their own mixture of problems, but these are found in rather less concentrated form. Nevertheless, we are left with the puzzling conclusion that the same contingency works in different ways upon different types of authorities.

The impact of resource instability was examined in the shire counties and the metropolitan authorities: the shire districts were excluded from the analysis because of the nature of the operational measure. Instability was found to affect the shire counties only, producing in those authorities a lower rate of differentiation. Counties that have suffered an unstable supply of resources since 1974 have found it more expedient to operate through fewer committees and departments than have those authorities of similar type with a greater certainty of resource supply. No such pattern is found in the metropolitan authorities.

Taking these results as a whole the important conclusion that should be drawn is that the environmental characteristics of a local authority are important determinants of its structural form. This is especially true of the range of environmental problems: the complexity of problems impacts upon the structures of all types of authorities. It is rather less true of environmental rsources although even here specific effects can be observed.

ORGANIZATIONAL CHARACTERISTICS

The size or scale of a local authority, as indicated by the number of councillors, or of employees, is also an important determinant of structure. Its effects are almost as widespread as those created by the range of environmental problems. However, the range and direction of the effects of size vary by type of authority. The shire counties respond to size by increasing the rates of differentiation, and of integration, and by developing a de-concentrated style of co-ordination. The shire districts are rather similar, except that the style of integration in these authorities remains unaffected. Larger districts tend to employ more committees, sub-committees, and departments and use more formal mechanisms for co-ordination. Metropolitan authorities are different again: they share some of the characteristics of the shire counties, and some of the shire districts. Larger metropolitan districts tend to be more differentiated (as in the counties and shire districts), but more concentrated in approach, and less formally integrated.

Political factors also affect local authority structures. In the shire districts a greater measure of political organization produces greater numbers of service *and* co-ordinating committees and departments, but has no effect upon integrative style. In the metropolitan authorities the same effect is noted on the extent of structural integration (high political organization produces high integration) but the extent of differentiation is untouched. Political organization in the counties affects the extent and style of integration. The more politically organized the county the more structurally integrated it is inclined to be, and it will operate through a de-concentrated style.

The political complexion of the council is of greater importance than its political organization as indicated by the strength of association. In the shire counties party control has a marked effect upon the extent of differentiation, with Labour authorities having significantly greater numbers of committees and sub-committees. A second, if more modest, effect is upon the extent of integration. Labour-controlled counties tend to have more integrative machinery. The metropolitan districts also demonstrate a strong association between Labour control and members of committees, sub-committees and departments. Labour-controlled metropolitan authorities, in other words, are the more differentiated. In the shire districts there is little difference in the structures of Labour and Conservative authorites, but there is a tendency for authorities with a large proportion of Independents to be less differentiated. Taking together the two aspects of accountability, it is interesting to note that in the shire counties and metropolitan authorities, all three aspects of structures are affected by party control *or* political organization, but not necessarily by both.

Finally, there is the impact of functional diversity. The importance of this contingency was examined by comparing the structures of the various types of local authorities. It was admitted that the operational measure lacked a degree of sensitivity and that the results would be rather tentative. Nevertheless, it seems that functional diversity (the range of functional responsibilities) affects the extent of differentiation but leaves the extent and style of integration untouched. The more the range of functions for which the authority has responsibility the greater will be the number of service committees and departments.

We have thus identified four organizational characteristics that are important determinants of organizational form. The effect of each, however, has been shown to vary according to type of authority. Hence, the overriding conclusion must be that the organizational characteristics of a local authority *are* important for its structural form but the precise nature of the relationship is dependent upon the type of authority. The effects of particular organizational characteristics are specific, and vary by type of authority. In one sense this confirms one of our underlying themes in that it demonstrates that structures and procedures can only be understood in relation to the peculiar blend of local circumstances. We have listed a number of organizational contingencies that are important in different ways in certain types of authorities.

Having identified associations between contingencies and structure it is possible to explain the recurrence of structural reorganization. One possibility is that an authority may be poorly adapted to its situation and seek a more appropriate match. To overcome the stresses and strains created by a lack of fit between structures and circumstance an authority may institute organizational review. This line of explanation is particularly relevant to many of the changes considered and introduced in the immediate post-1974 years. The new local authorities were too influenced by the diagrammatic analysis presented in the Bains Report, and as a consequence designed structures out of step with the requirements of environment, organization scale, and so on. There has been an inevitable reconsideration of the structures introduced in 1973-4. Such an approach, however, could lead to the misleading conclusion that authorities can avoid further internal reorganization once the influence of Bains has been removed. If only the authority can find an appropriate form of organization — appropriate, that is, for its environmental and organizational characteristics — then change would be unnecessary. Such an aspiration is unlikely to be fulfilled, for two reasons. First, the contingencies themselves are not stable, but liable to change. We have already seen, in the past five or six years, significant changes in the incidence of political organization, and in the complexion of many local councils. Both these organizational characteristics are related to structural form. We have also seen a greater instability in the supply of resources — a trend likely to persist. This contingency is also associated with various structural arrangements. Over a longer period we may well experience changes in the remaining contingencies. The altering composition and distribution of the population (Central Policy Review Staff, 1977; Solace, 1978) may well reshape the range and form of environmental problems experienced in particular localities. In short, local authorities have already experienced, and will continue to experience, changes in significant contingencies which will require organizational adjustment.

Much of the above repeats the arguments stated in Chapter 5. But there is a third explanation of recurring organizational change — the existence of contradictory contingencies. Chapter 6 pointed to the dilemma facing a number of authorities whose contingencies operate in different directions. A large shire county, for example, under the control of the Conservative Party, would be in such a position. The pressures of scale would be for increased differentiation and integration; the pressures of party control would be for low differentiation and low integration. Inherent in the mix of contingencies are the causes of organizational instability and change. In endeavouring to manage the inconsistent impulses from a range of environmental and organizational contingencies, authorities may seek periodic organizational review.

The data in Chapters 4 and 6 do meet the aims of the present study. The former describes the variation that exists and in a manner amenable to theoretical explanation. The latter demonstrates the utility of contingency theory as a vehicle for explaining that variation, and for suggesting expectations of change. In the following section, therefore, we shall consider how a contingency analysis of local authority practices can be extended and developed. The particular expression of contingency theory provided in earlier chapters has limitations and could be improved. Having satisfied ourselves of the important contribution that is provided by contingency theory, it is perhaps worth suggesting ways in which the present model could be refined. Finally, we shall point to one of the crucial gaps in the contingency approach, and make the case for complementary studies of organizational behaviour. In doing so our purpose is to sharpen the boundaries of contingency theory, thus exposing its principal strengths and weaknesses.

DEVELOPMENT OF THE FRAMEWORK

Any attempt to explain events or occurrences — in the present case, local authority management structures — involves the construction of a conceptual framework, and the preparation of causal narratives linking two or more concepts. The initial strength of a theory is dependent upon the clarity of the conceptual framework and the conviction of narratives. But all theories in the social sciences are limited, in that they are unable to explain fully the events observed. In our case we have explained some of the variations in management structures, but there is still variation that cannot be explained in terms of the contingencies explored here. From one point of view the conceptual framework prepared in Chapter 5 has been comparatively successful. The amount of variation explained (Table 7.2) is encouraging. The extents of differentiation and integration are substantially influenced by the environmental and organizational characteristics discussed, but the extent of concentration less so. These figures demonstrate, however, that there are other factors which determine the structures of local authorities. In particular, the style of integration appears relatively unrelated to environmental and organizational characteristics. The evident question, therefore, is what are these other factors and how can they be incorporated into the contingency framework?

TABLE 7.2   *Amount of Variation Explained by Type of Authority* [a]

Authority	Extent of differentiation	Extent of integration	Style of integration
Shire counties	36%	48%	9%
Metropolitan districts	51%	20%	12%
Shire districts	30%	22%	5%

[a] Amount explained (R^2).

One possibility is to identify further contingencies, that is, constraints acting upon the local authority. At least two sets of contingencies may be important. First, there is the pattern of demand articulation which was raised in an earlier chapter as an important characteristic of the environment, although not studied here because of the lack of suitable operational measures. Secondly, and perhaps more importantly, there is the role of ideas. Local authorities are set within a world of ideas which have a direct relevance for their structure and functioning. The historical review presented in Chapter 2 traced the influence of ideas expressed by a series of national reports. We have made several references to the influence of the Bains Working Group who themselves were influenced by the principles and practice of the 'corporate approach'. Such an approach, if accepted, leads to acceptance of certain structural forms and the rejection of others. The Birmingham document cited at the beginning of Chapter 5 illustrates how different ideas about the management of a local authority have different structural implications. Other examples in rather different contexts, of the relationship between ideas and structure include Sloan (1963), Chandler (1962) and Warwick (1975). The extent to which contingency theory could explain structural variation and change would no doubt be enhanced through inclusion of ideological contingencies within the conceptual framework.

Attempts to make the list of contingencies comprehensive would offer a second possibility of development. Contingencies have usually been presented (as here) as though they were unrelated. In fact they are interrelated. For example, the contingencies covered in our study are related as shown in Figure 7.1.*

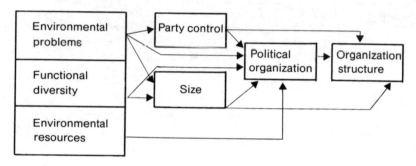

FIGURE 7.1

The model assumes that organizational characteristics (party control, political organization, size) are dependent upon, rather than determinants of, environmental factors. From that assumption a number of relationships may be traced. Thus, the greater the range of environmental problems the more likely that the Labour Party will hold a high proportion of council seats. This is not a particularly contentious statement. It means little more, for example, than that the Conservative Party is unlikely to secure control of Tower Hamlets, whereas the Labour Party is unlikely to gain Solihull. Certain kinds of environment produce particular

*The path coefficients relevant to the diagram are not provided. The linkages given are based on path coefficients greater than twice their standard error.

Also excluded are the direct links between, on the one hand, environmental problems, functional diversity and environmental resources, and on the other, organization structure.

patterns of voting. Political organization, on the other hand, is rather more complex. It is affected by several factors. Political organization represents an attempt to control the policies and decisions of the local authority. But the need for such control occurs more readily in some circumstances than others. Thus, a range of pressing environmental problems may provide the stimulus for elected representatives to structure and control the activities of the bureaucracy. The acuteness and complexity of environmental problems produces a rationale and argument for co-ordinated action directed by organized and co-ordinated groups of political representatives. Hence the link between range of environmental problems and political organization. The same argument could be made concerning the range of functions provided by the authority. The greater the functional diversity the greater the need for co-ordinated member behaviour. In a metropolitan district, for example, problems of housing interact with problems of residential provision for old people (reflecting the range of environmental problems), both of which are services within the responsibility of the authority (functional diversity) and require a co-ordinated approach (political organization).

It is unnecessary to unravel other links in the above diagram. The examples cited so far are sufficient to illustrate that contingencies are interrelated. We would suggest that analysis of interactions between contingencies offers the possibility of theoretical advance. To learn how contingencies operate both directly upon management structures (as explored in Chapter 6) and *indirectly* through one another would provide a more sophisticated form of analysis and theory. An essential methodological requirement of such a multivariate approach, however, is the inclusion of a comparatively exhaustive list of contingent factors; otherwise the associations between the various contingencies become theoretically difficult to interpret (Blalock, 1971). The inclusion of variables such as demand articulation and ideologies, however, may move us towards the position where multivariate analysis becomes appropriate.

The third development within the framework of contingency theory concerns the study of local authority performance. Underlying contingency theory is the assumption that the congruence between structures and contingencies *matters*. An organization with a strategy relevant to its situational circumstances is more likely to provide effective performance than if the strategy were inappropriate. In early work this key assumption was explicitly advanced. Weber (1947) associated bureaucratic control strategies with 'purely technical superiority'. Similarly, Woodward (1958), Stinchcombe (1959) and Burns and Stalker (1961) each demonstrated how the association between certain contingencies and organizational structures affected performance. In contrast, later papers have tended to ignore performance. The focus of inquiry has shifted towards the interaction of structure with contingencies, and away from the interactions of structure and contingencies with performance.

Our suggestion would be that contingency theory should bring analysis of performance within its focus. Analytically it is legitimate to separate the study of how structures are affected by contingencies from the study of the consequences of those structures. But, the fundamental persuasion of contingency theory leads to consideration of performance, and future studies should advance in that direction. Having made that point, it is worth adding a cautionary note. Performance is difficult to define. Steers (1975) in his review of seventeen important studies into organizational effectiveness identifies at least fourteen possible measures. The initial conclusion (from Steers) is that an organization may be effective when assessed in terms of one yardstick, but ineffective in terms of others. In short, how well a local authority has a 'goodness of fit' between its management structure and situational contingencies depends largely on the evaluation criteria being used. With one set of criteria an organization may have a good fit, and at the same time have a bad fit when assessed according to a different set of criteria. It is easy to picture the situation where the political goals may be inconsistent with the economic goals of efficiency. In order to secure participation by elected representatives, and to facilitate their control over decisions, the routing of information and the location of influence and authority over decisions may well be different from what it would be if speed and efficiency were the only considerations.

We are suggesting that contingency theory should have a wider conceptual and empirical base than has been prevalent in recent years (and than exists in the present study). It should seek to determine how the associations between structures and contingencies affect performance, thus allowing fuller expression of the logical structure of the contingency approach. However, care must be taken to recognize that the concept of performance is complex, involving several, sometimes unconnected dimensions. Performance, like structure, is a multi-dimensional concept. We need to know not only *why* alternative strategies are adopted but the *full range* of their performance consequences.

ORGANIZATIONAL BEHAVIOUR AND THE ROLE OF CHOICE

Contingency theory seeks to explain the nature of organizational structures and practices in terms of environmental and organizational characteristics. There is a strong tendency towards an impersonal and mechanistic form of explanation, ignoring the role played by organizational actors. Such a statement requires clarification. Many writers normally included as contributing to the development of contingency theory *were* concerned with the role played by organizational actors. Burns and Stalker (1961), for example, emphasize that the perceptions of organizational members play a crucial role in mediating the impact of the environment on the organization. Lawrence and Lorsch (1967) are also concerned with the orientations of actors within the organization. But the predominant mode of research within the contingency framework has emphasized relationships between context and organizational structure without reference to the importance of actors within the organization.

The argument of contingency theory is that for an organization to perform effectively its structure must 'fit' its circumstances. But the degree of 'fit' manifestly varies. Some organizations 'fit' their context rather better than others; organizations do not adapt, mechanically, to their contexts. Some organizations do not adapt, others do so but in various ways. Therefore, it is necessary to ask *why* some organizations change their management structures in response to changed circumstances while others do not. Burns and Stalker (1961) would argue, correctly in our view, that to answer that question requires attention to organizational processes, that is, the processes whereby actors within an authority interpret their situational circumstances and seek to develop appropriate responses. In other words, some consideration must be given to the *politics* of organizational behaviour. The relationship between an organization and its context is not one of mechanical adaptation. People within an organization can influence its structure and process. It is they who have to understand which contingencies are creating stresses and strains, and it is they who have to make choices as to what might be an appropriate form of organization. Contingencies impose constraints, but 'choices' have to be made.

The importance of the process of choice for an understanding of why local authorities develop as they do, is highlighted when it is remembered that organizational actors do not necessarily interpret *in the same way* the constraints of the environment and the organizational context. Different actors may wish to structure an organization in different ways. To understand why the management structure of Birmingham in 1980 is different from that which existed in 1974, and different again from those in Liverpool, Leeds and Manchester, it is important to know something about how key politicians, and officers, regard alternative systems of management. Any management system affects the distribution of scarce and valued organizational resources. The creation of a directorate system may affect the status and influence of subordinated professions; policy committees may restrict the role and opportunities of backbench members; chief executives and management teams may circumscribe the status and autonomy of chief officers, determine the role of committees, and threaten the influence and control of the party leadership. To reduce numbers of committees and departments might be to reduce the career opportunities of professional officers, and at the same time to limit the proportion of members who can become chairmen of committees. In other words, management structures have consequences for the distribution of valued but limited resources.

Any management system is regarded by officers and members as a vehicle threatening or maintaining the existing distribution of resources. Therefore, officers and members will be committed or resistant to the existing management structure, and to any proposed or conceivable changes. Disaffected individuals and groups will seek to alter an unsatisfactory (to them) management system, and to replace it with arrangements more consistent with their interests. Favoured individuals and groups, on the other hand, will seek to retain existing arrangements. A local authority, like all organizations, may be thought of as a federation of individuals and groups, each with distinguishable interests, seeking to further those interests through creation of a management system consistent with those interests. Groups struggle to determine the form of the management system.

The local authority is not, therefore, a passive system upon which external forces (contingencies) impact. There is a process of mediation between organization and environment in which actors seek to further their interests. *Whether* an authority responds to situational contingencies, *to which* contingencies it responds and *in what manner*, is a function of the internal processes of struggle and mediation. But, we would emphasize that the struggle is constrained by external contingencies. To paraphrase a famous dictum: 'men make their own organizations but not under circumstances of their own choosing.' The organizational structure of any local authority is the product of constrained choice. Contingent factors impose constraint within which members and officers struggle to choose how they should and shall be organized.

It is interesting to note that there may be greater latitude for choice in some areas than in others. The analysis of earlier chapters would suggest that the extents of organizational differentiation and integration are more constrained than is the style of integration. The relationships found between contingencies and the extents of differentiation and integration were stronger than those for the style of integration: this implies that local authorities are more constrained in the way they divide up their work and in the extent of their integrative machinery, than in how that machinery is operated. It may be that this is the result of the comparatively recent emphasis placed upon the need for integration. There is a long tradition of structuring local authorities along professional lines. That is, the process of differentiation is largely established. The arguments for integration, however, are more recent, and more disputed. The relatively recent emphasis upon the ideas of integration is still a matter of dispute: hence the style of integration adopted is a response to internal politics and not to situational contingencies. The exigencies of environment and organization are ignored. Over time, however, the advantages or strains of particular styles may become more apparent and authorities may find it convenient to adapt rather more to their situation. In short, the degree of choice currently exercised over the appropriate style of integration may become rather more constrained.

The process of choice is also crucial wherever an authority is faced with *conflicting* contingencies. Contingencies impacting upon a local authority do not necessarily work in the same direction. Several examples of this situation were noted in Chapter 6. Authorities of this kind have to choose to which contingencies they will adapt, and which are to be ignored.

It is beyond the purpose of our study to pursue further the process of choice, or the interaction of contingencies and choice. Our purpose has been to identify the nature of the constraints that exist and to establish the structural consequence of those constraints. We would not argue that the relationship between the organization and the environment is a purely mechanistic one and have admitted the importance of organizational choice. Indeed, our later work (Ranson *et al.*, 1980) has begun to tease out the operation of mediation and choice under different conditions. Nevertheless, the organizational pattern adopted by a local authority *is* the result of members of the organization acting *within a set of environmental and organizational constraints.* Our purpose has been to identify those constraints and the nature of their effect. In other words, to raise the importance of 'choice' is not to deny the importance of contingency theory. Contingency analysis of the form presented here is an essential prerequisite to the study of how actors within an authority manipulate the process of choice.

References

Aldrich, H. and S. Mindlin (1978) Uncertainty and dependence: two perspectives on environment. In Karpik (ed.), *Organization and Environment.* London: Sage.

Aldrich, H. A. (1976) Resource dependence and interorganizational relations. *Administration and Society,* February 1976.

Aldrich, H. A. and J. Pfeffer (1976) Environments of organizations. *Annual Review of Sociology 2.*

Anderson, T. and S. Warkov (1961) Organizational size and functional complexity. *American Sociological Review,* February 1961.

Bains Working Group (1972) *The New Local Authorities. Management and Structure.* London: H.M.S.O.

Baker, R. J. S. (1972) *Administrative Theory and Public Administration.* London: Hutchinson.

Baldridge, J. V. (1971) *Power and Conflict in the University.* Chichester: Wiley.

Basildon UDC (1966) The Basildon experiment. *Public Administration.* Summer 1966.

Benson, J. K. (1975) The interorganizational network as a political economy. *Administrative Science Quarterly.* June 1975.

Blalock, H. M. (ed.) (1971) *Causal Models in the Social Sciences.* London: Macmillan.

Blau, P. M. (1968) The hierarchy of authority in organizations. *American Journal of Sociology.* January 1968.

Blau, P. M. and R. Schoenherr (1971) *The Structure of Organizations.* New York: Basic Books.

Blau, P. M., C. McHugh Falbe, W. McKinley and P. K. Tracy (1976) Technology and organization in manufacturing. *Administrative Science Quarterly.* March 1976.

Blauner, R. (1964) *Alienation and Freedom.* University of Chicago Press.

Boaden, N. T. (1971) *Urban Policy-Making.* Cambridge University Press.

Bosworth, N. B. A. (1976) *A Revised System of Management and Officer Structure.* Report to Finance and Priorities (Ad Hoc) Sub-Committee, November 1976.

Brown, R.G.S. (1970) *The Administrative Process in Britain.* London: Methuen.

Bulpitt, J. G. (1967) *Party Politics in English Local Government.* London: Longman.

173

Burns, T. (1977) *The BBC: Public Institution and Private World*. London: Macmillan.

Burns, T. and G. M. Stalker (1961) *The Management of Innovation*. London: Tavistock.

Butt, R. B. (1972) A feasibility study of PPBS in Gloucestershire. *Local Government Studies*. April 1972.

Central Policy Review Staff (1977) *Population and the Social Services*. London: H.M.S.O.

Chandler, Alfred D. Jr. (1962) *Strategy and Structure*. Cambridge, Mass.: M.I.T. Press.

Chester, D. N. (1968) Local Democracy and the internal organization of local authorities. *Public Administration,* Autumn 1968.

Child, J. (1972) Organization structure, environment and performance — The role of strategic choice. *Sociology,* January 1972.

Child, J. (1973) Predicting and understanding organization structure. *Administrative Science Quarterly,* June 1973.

Committee on Management of Local Government (1967). *Report. Volumes 1-5*. London: H.M.S.O.

Corina, L. (1977) *Local Government Decision Making: Some Influences on Elected Members' Role Playing*. Papers in Community Studies, Department of Social Administration and Social Work, University of York.

Coventry CBC (1954) Coventry and organization and methods. *Public Administration*. Spring 1954.

Cross, J. A. (1970) *British Public Administration*. University Tutorial Press.

Davies, Jon Gower (1972) *The Evangelistic Bureaucrat. A Study of a Planning Exercise in Newcastle upon Tyne*. London: Tavistock.

Dearlove, John (1973) *The Politics of Policy in Local Government*. Cambridge University Press.

Donoughue, B. and G. W. Jones (1973) *Professional Politician: The Life of Herbert Morrison 1888-1965*. London: Weidenfeld and Nicholson.

Downey, H. K., D. H. Hellriegel and J. W. Stocum Jr. (1975) Environmental uncertainty: The construct and its application. *Administrative Science Quarterly*. December 1975.

Dunsire, A. (1973) *Administration, The Word and the Science*. Oxford: Martin Robertson.

Eddison, P.A. (1973) *Local Government: Management and Corporate Planning*. Leonard Hill.

Elkin, S. (1974) *Politics and Land Use Planning. The London Experience*. Cambridge University Press.

Elliott, J. (1971) The Harris experiment in Newcastle upon Tyne. *Public Administration*. Summer 1971.

Elliott, J. (1975) Political leadership in local government: T. Dan Smith in Newcastle upon Tyne. *Local Government Studies*. April 1975.

Faunce, W. (1968) *Problems of an Industrial Society*. New York: McGraw-Hill.

Fiske, D. (1975) *Education — The Cuckoo in the Local Government*

Nest. Lady Simon of Wythenshawe Memorial Lecture.

Franko, L. G. (1974) The move toward a multidivisional structure in European organizations. *Administrative Science Quarterly.* December 1974.

Garner, J. F. (1973) The "Ultra Vires" doctrine and the local government Bill. *Local Government Studies.* February 1973.

Grant, W. (1977) *Independent Local Politics in England and Wales.* Farnborough: D.C. Heath — Saxon House Studies.

Greenwood, R. (1978) Politics and public bureaucracies: A reconsideration. *Policy and Politics.* June 1978.

Greenwood, R. and C. R. Hinings (1976) Contingency theory and public bureaucracies. *Policy and Politics.* December 1976.

Greenwood, R., C. R. Hinings and S. Ranson (1975) Contingency theory and the organization of local authorities: Part 1, Differentiation and integration. *Public Administration.* Spring 1975.

Greenwood, R., C. R. Hinings and S. Ranson (1977) The politics of the budgetary process in English local government. *Political Studies 25.* March 1977.

Greenwood, R., C. R. Hinings, S. Ranson and K. Walsh (1979) Incremental budgeting and the assumption of growth: the experience of local government: 1974-8. In M. Wright (ed.) *Public Spending Decisions: Growth and Restraint in the 1970s.* London: Allen and Unwin.

Greenwood, R., A. L. Norton and J. D. Stewart (1969) Recent changes in the internal organization of county boroughs: Part 1: Committees, Part 2: Delegation and Departmental Reorganization. *Public Administration.* Summer, Autumn 1969.

Greenwood, R., A. D. Smith, and J. D. Stewart (1971) *New Patterns of Local Government Organization.* Occasional Paper, Institute of Local Government Studies.

Greenwood, R. and J. D. Stewart (1973) Towards a typology of English local authorities *Political Studies.* March 1973.

Greenwood, R. and J. D. Stewart (1974) *Corporate Planning in English Local Government.* London: Charles Knight.

Greenwood, R., J. D. Stewart and A. D. Smith (1972) The policy committee in English local government. *Public Administration.* Summer 1972.

Hage, J. (1978) Toward a synthesis of the dialectic between historical-specific and sociological-general models of the environment. In Karpik (ed.) *Organization and Environment,* pp. 103-45. London: Sage.

Hage, J. and M. Aiken (1967) Relationship of centralization to other structural properties. *Administrative Science Quarterly.* June 1967.

Hage, J. and M. Aiken (1969) Routine technology, social structure and organizational goals. *Administrative Science Quarterly.* September 1969.

Hall, R. H. (1962) Interorganizational structural variation: application of the bureaucratic model. *Administrative Science Quarterly.* December 1962.

Hall, R. H. (1963) The concept of bureaucracy: an empirical assessment. *American Journal of Sociology.* July 1963.

Hambleton, R. (1977) Policies for areas. *Local Government Studies.* April 1977.

Hambleton, R. (1978) *Policy Planning and Local Government.* London: Hutchinson.

Hampton, W. (1970) *Democracy and Community. A Study of Politics in Sheffield.* Oxford University Press

Hansard (1976) Chief Education Officer, 8 November 1976, pp. 197-186.

Haynes, R. J. (1978) The rejection of corporate management in Birmingham in theoretical perspective. *Local Government Studies.* April 1978.

Haywood, S. (1977) Decision-making in local government — the case of an "Independent" council. *Local Government Studies.* October 1977.

Heydebrand, W. V. (1973) *Hospital Bureaucracy: A Comparative Study of Organizations.* Dunellen.

Hickson, D. J., D. S. Pugh and D. C. Pheysey (1969) Operations technology and organization structure: a reappraisal. *Administrative Science Quarterly.* September 1969.

Hinings, C. R., R. Greenwood and S. Ranson (1975) Contingency theory and the organization of local authorities: Part 2 contingencies and structure. *Public Administration.* Summer 1975.

Hinings, C.R., R. Greenwood, S. Ranson and K. Walsh (1979) The organizational consequences of inflation in English local government. In M. Wright (ed.) *Public Spending Decisions: Growth and Restraint in the 1970s.* London: Allen and Unwin.

Hinings, C.R., R. Greenwood, S. Ranson and K. Walsh (1980) *The Management Structures of Local Authorities.* London: H.M.S.O., in press.

Jackman, R. and M. Sellars (1977) The Distribution of RSG: the hows and whys of the new needs formula *CES Review* July 1977.

Jackson, R. M. (1965) *The Machinery of Local Government,* 2nd edn. London: Macmillan.

Jenkins, R. (1971) The reality of political power. *Sunday Times.* 17 January 1971.

Jenkins, W. I. (1978) *Policy Analysis: A Political and Organisational Perspective.* Oxford: Martin Robertson.

Jennings, R. E. (1975) Political perspectives on local government reorganization. *Local Government Studies.* October 1975.

Jennings, R. E. (1977) *Education and Politics.* London: Batsford

Jones, G. W. (1973) Political leadership in local government: how Herbert Morrison governed London, 1934-1940. *Local Government Studies.* June 1973.

Karpik, L. (ed.) (1978) *Organization and Environment. Theory, Issues and Reality.* London: Sage.

Kast, F. R. and J. E. Rosenzweig (1973) *Contingency Views of Organization and Management.* Henley-on-Thames: Science Research Associates.

Kimberly, J. R. (1976) Organization size and the structuralist perspective: a review, critique and proposal. *Administrative Science Quarterly.* December 1976.

Kinch, M.B. (1974) Departmental reorganization in a local authority, *Public Administration*. Spring 1974.

Knowles, R. S. (1977) *Modern Management in Local Government*. Barry Rose (second edition)

Lawrence, P. R. and J. W. Lorsch (1967) *Organization and Environment*. Harvard University Press.

Landsberger, Henry A. (1961) The horizontal dimension in a bureaucracy. *Administrative Science Quarterly*. December 1961.

Lee, J. M., Bruce Wood, B. W. Solomon and P. Walters (1974) *The Scope of Local Initiative. A Study of Cheshire County Council*. Oxford: Martin Robertson.

Litwak, E. (1961) Models of bureaucracy which permit conflict, *American Journal of Sociology*. September 1961.

Lomer, M. A. (1977) The chief executive in local government 1974-6. *Local Government Studies*. October 1977.

Long, J. (1975) The impact of scale on management structures and processes. *Local Government Studies*. April 1975.

Long, J. and P. Richer (1968) *Administration in a Large Local Authority: A Comparison with other County Boroughs*. London: HMSO.

Lupton, T. (1971) *Management and the Social Services*, 2nd edn. Harmondsworth: Penguin.

Lynch, B. and M. Perlman (1978) Local authority predictions of expenditure and income. *CES Review*, May 1978.

McKinsey and Co. Inc. (1971) *Hull — A Turning Point*. In R. Greenwood and J. D. Stewart (eds.) *Corporate Planning in English Local Government*. Tonbridge: Charles Knight.

McNeil, K. (1978) Understanding organizational power: building on the Weberian legacy. *Administrative Science Quarterly*. March 1978.

Mason, T. (1978) Area management — the progress of an idea in local government organization. *Local Government Studies*. January 1978.

Meyer, M. W. (1972) *Bureaucratic Structure and Authority: Co-ordination and Control in 254 Government Agencies*. London: Harper and Row.

Moser, C. A. and W. Scott (1961) *British Towns*. Edinburgh: Oliver and Boyd.

Newton, K. (1976) *Second City Politics — Democratic Process and Decision Making in Birmingham*. Oxford: Clarendon Press.

Ostergaard, G. N. (1954) Labour and the public corporation. *The Manchester School*. May 1954.

Page, H. (1936) *Co-ordination and Planning in the Local Authority*. Manchester University Press

Paterson Advisory Group (1973) *The New Scottish Local Authorities Organization and Management Structures*. London: H.M.S.O.

Perrow, C. (1967) A framework for the comparative analysis of organizations. *American Sociological Review*. April 1967.

Pettigrew, A. (1973) *The Politics of Organizational Decision-Making*. London: Tavistock.

Pugh, D. S. (1971) *Organization Theory*. Harmondsworth: Penguin.

Pugh, D. S., D. J. Hickson, C. R. Hinings and C. Turner (1969) The context of organization structure. *Administrative Science Quarterly.* March 1969.

Ranson, S., C.R. Hinings and R. Greenwood (1980) The structuring of organization structure. *Administrative Science Quarterly,* in press.

Redcliffe-Maud, Ld. and B. Wood (1974) *English Local Government Reformed.* London: Oxford University Press.

Rhodes, R. A. W. (1975) *A Comparative Model of British Local Politics.* Institute of Local Government Studies, University of Birmingham, unpublished.

Richards, P. G. (1968) *The New Local Government System.* London: Allen and Unwin.

Richards, P. G. (1973) *The Reformed Local Government System.* London: Allen and Unwin.

Ridley, F. F. (1975) *The Study of Government: Political Science and Public Administration.* London: Allen and Unwin.

Rowan, P. (1977) Beleaguered by Bains and bureaucrats. *Times Educational Supplement.* 18 March 1977, 25 March 1977.

Royal Commission on Local Government in England, 1966-1969 (1969) *Volume 1 Report.* London: H.M.S.O.

Saunders, P. (1974) *Who Runs Croydon? Power and Politics in a London Borough.* Doctoral thesis, University of London.

Schoderbek, P. B. (ed.) (1971) *Management Systems.* Chichester: Wiley.

Self, P. J. O. (1972) *Administrative Theories and Politics.* London: Allen and Unwin.

Sharpe, L. J. (1970) Theories and values of local government. *Political Studies.* June 1970.

Skinner, D. and J. Langdon (1974) *The Story of Clay Cross.* Spokesman Books.

Skitt, J. (ed.) (1975) *Practical Corporate Planning in Local Government* London: Leonard Hill.

Sloan, Alfred P. Jr. (1963) *My Years with General Motors.* London: Sidgwick and Jackson.

Smith T. Dan (1965) Local government in Newcastle upon Tyne. *Public Administration.* Winter 1965.

Society of Local Authority Chief Executives (1978) *Population Change and Local Government.* Society of Local Authority Chief Executives.

Steers, R. M. (1975) Problems in the measurement of organizational effectiveness. *Administrative Science Quarterly.* December 1975.

Stewart, J. D. (1970) *Local Authority Policy Planning.* Local Government Chronicle. London: Charles Knight.

Stewart, J. D. (1971) *Management in Local Government: a Viewpoint.* London: Charles Knight.

Stewart, J.D., K. Spencer and B. Webster (1976) *Local Government Approaches to Urban Deprivation.* London: Home Office.

Stinchcombe, A. L. (1959) Bureaucratic and craft administration of production: a comparative study. *Administrative Science Quarterly.* September 1959.

Strauss, G. (1962) Tactics of lateral relationship: the purchasing agent.

Administrative Science Quarterly. September 1962.

Sutcliffe, A. S. (1976) Political leadership in labour-controlled Birmingham. *Local Government Studies.* January 1976.

Sutcliffe, A. and R. Smith (1974) *Birmingham 1939-70.* Oxford University Press.

Tivey, L. J. (1966) *Nationalisation in British Industry.* London: Jonathan Cape.

Urwick Orr and Partners Ltd. (1972) *Proposals for reorganization at Walsall.* In R. Greenwood and J. D. Stewart (eds.) *Corporate Planning in English Local Government.* London: Charles Knight.

Walker, C. J. and R. H. Guest (1952) *The Man on the Assembly Line.* Harvard University Press.

Walton R. E. and J. M. Dutton (1969) The management of interdepartmental conflict: a model and review. *Administrative Science Quarterly.* March 1969.

Warwick, D. P. (1975) *A Theory of Public Bureaucracy.* Harvard Press.

Wates, N. (1976) *The Battle for Tolmers Square.* London: Routledge and Kegan Paul.

Webber, R. and J. Craig (1976) Which authorities are alike? *Population Trends.* No. 5, Autumn 1976.

Weber M. (1947) *The Theory of Social and Economic Organization* (trans. A. M. Henderson and T. Parsons). Oxford University Press.

Webster, B. and J. D. Stewart (1974) The Area Analysis of Resources *Policy and Politics.* September 1974.

Whisler, T. L. (1970) *Information Technology and Organizational Change.* Wadsworth.

Wiseman, H. V. (1963) The working of local government in Leeds. *Public Administration.* Spring and Summer 1963.

Woodward, J. (1958) *Management and Technology.* London: H.M.S.O.

Woodward, J. (1965) *Industrial Organization.* Oxford University Press.

Wright, M.W. (1980) *Public Spending Decisions: Growth and Restraint in the 1970s.* London: Allen and Unwin.

Zald, M. N. (1970) Political economy: a framework for comparative analysis. In M. N. Zald (ed.) *Power in Organizations.* Vanderbilt University Press.

Zwerman, W. L. (1970) *New Perspectives on Organization Theory.* Greenwood.

Index

accountability, 73-4, 90
  civil-service model of, 73-4, 75, 79
  local government model of, 73-4
administrative coordination, 20-1
administrative efficiency, 21
Aiken, M., 110, 115
Aldrich, H.A., 100, 103
Alnwick, 147
Anderson, T., 116
architectural services, 18, 25, 41
area approaches, 4, 42-3, 45, 93
art galleries, 18

Bains Working Group, 5, 12-13, 28, 30, 36, 38-41, 45-6, 49-50, 53, 55, 75-6, 84-5, 86, 94, 97-9, 163, 165
Baldridge, J.V., 112
Baker, R.J.S., 9
Basildon, 2
Benson, J.K., 103
Birmingham, 55, 92-4, 96-7, 99, 107, 165, 170
Blackpool, 102
Blalock, H.M., 167
Blau, P.M., 109, 112
Blauner, R., 115
Boaden, N.T., 100
Bosworth, N.B.A., 92-5, 97-8
Bradford, 94, 96
Brighton, 96, 102
Bristol, 96, 146
Brown, R.G.S., 9

Bulpitt, J.G., 121
Burns, T., 100, 112, 115, 168, 169
Butt, R.B., 40

central-local relations, 14
Central Policy Review Staff, 163
Chandler, A.D., 107, 166
Chester, D.N., 30
chief executive, 2-4, 6, 12, 19-20, 23-4, 26, 28-9, 38, 45, 48-51, 53-63, 76-80, 81-5, 87, 89, 94-5, 105, 107, 111, 122
Child, J., 8, 112, 129
child care, 15
clerk, 19, 20, 28, 48-9, 55, 87
clerk's department, 15, 23, 25, 85
Committee on Management of Local Government, 5, 11, 12-31 passim, 33-6, 39, 43, 48, 50, 64, 82, 89, 112, 123, 143
comprehensive education, 119
computers, 115
Congleton, 96
consumer protection, 39, 130
Conservative Party, 54, 92, 98, 121-3, 130, 132, 143-5, 149-50, 162-3, 166
contingency theory, 7-10 95-172 passim
Corina, L., 108
Cornwall, 150
corporate, approach, 5, 38, 45-6, 52, 54, 90, 92-4, 107, 165

181

groups, *see* interdepartmental
        groups
management, 22, 56, 92, 107
planning, 6, 21-2, 46, 50, 52,
        54-5, 77, 80, 85-6, 122
council, 59, 60, 80, 108
county, authority, 17, 35, 114
    see also shire county
            metropolitan county
    borough, 17, 20, 35, 112-14,
        121
Coventry, 16, 22-7 *passim*
Craig, J., 128
Cross, J.A., 2
Cumbria, 55, 150
cuts, 56, 107

Davies, J.G., 108
Dearlove, J., 95, 100, 108, 121
delegation, 14
demand articulation, *see*
    environmental characteristics
democracy, 1
Derby, 151
differentiation, 9-10, 13, 17, 21,
        28, 33, 38, 40, 67-91 *passim,*
        96-7, 101-2, 106, 110-16
        passim, 125-6, 131-65
        passim
    extent of, 17-18, 30, 34-8, 65,
        131, 170
    criteria of, 18, 30, 39-47
directorate system, 28, 40-1
Dunsire, A., 9, 119
Dutton, J.M., 112
Dyfed, 150

economic criteria, 117-18
economics of scale, 15, 101
education, 3, 18, 24, 39, 41, 56, 81,
        92, 130
Eddison, P.A., 21
elections, 54
Elkin, S., 108
Elliot, J., 2, 16, 95, 121
engineering, 41
environment, 7, 90

environmental characteristics,
        100-10, 126-9, 158-61,
        169, 172
    problems, 100-3, 126-8, 132,
        134-55 *passim,* 166-7
    resources, 100, 103-8, 128-9,
        132, 134-55 *passim,*
        166-7
    stability of, 105-8, 128, 132,
        135-6, 137
    scale of (wealth), 103-5, 129,
        132, 135-7, 139-55
        passim
    demand articulation, 96, 100,
        108-9, 165, 167
environmental health, 18, 41-2,
        127, 130
estates, 24, 41, 113
executive office, 6, 23, 24, 29, 76
Exeter, 55

Faunce, W., 115
'federal' local authorities, 15-16
finance, 3, 72, 78, 84-5, 86
Finance and General Purposes
        Committee, 58
fire, 15, 39, 130
Fiske, D., 56
Franko, L.G., 117
functional diversity, *see*
        technology

Garner, J.F., 3
Gosport, 147
Grant, W., 146
Greenwood, R., 5, 10-11, 15-21,
        75, 121-2, 131
Guest, R.H., 115

Hage, J., 100, 110, 115
Hall, R.H., 110
Hambleton, R., 4
Hampton, W., 119
Hansard, 56
Harris, F., 16
Haynes, R.J., 2
Haywood, S., 2

health, 18, 24
Heydebrand, W.V., 112
Hickson, D.J., 115
highways, 15, 24, 56, 130, 134
Hinings, C.R., 10-11, 27, 54, 56,
　74, 121, 131, 157
Home Office, 118-19
hospitals, 116
housing, 18, 42, 81, 127, 129
Hall, 22-7 *passim*, 40

ideas (as a contingency), 165
Independents, 130, 149
"integral" local authority, 15-16,
　21
integration, 9-10, 13, 17, 28-9,
　33, 38, 67-90 *passim*, 95, 101,
　104, 106-7, 110-11, 114,
　116, 121, 123, 131-64 *passim*,
　165
　extent of, 22, 30, 48-57, 67-90
　　passim, 156
　style of, 22-7 *passim*, 29-30,
　　57-65, 67-90 *passim*,
　　113-14, 156
interdepartmental groups, 45, 47,
　51-2, 54, 56-7, 62-4, 67,
　78, 80-2, 84-5, 87, 89, 92,
　107, 114, 136

Jackman, R., 106, 129
Jackson, R.M., 2
Jenkins, Roy, 118-19
Jenkins, W.I., 100
Jennings, R.E., 74, 121
Jones, G.W., 95, 121

Kast, E.R., 7, 8
key issue analysis, 47
Kinch, M.B., 2
Knowles, R.S., 2

Labour Party, 98, 119, 121-3, 130,
　132, 143, 146, 149-50
　161-2, 166
land, 72, 79, 84-5
land-use planning, *see* planning

Langdon, J., 95
Landsberger, H.A., 112
Lawrence, P.R., 89, 115, 117, 119,
　169
Lee, J.M., 95
Leeds, 94, 170
legal-institutional approach, 2-5
leisure, *see* recreation
Liberal Party, 130, 143
libraries, 18, 39, 41, 56, 130
Litwak, E., 115
Liverpool, 5, 96, 170
Lomer, M.A., 4, 55
London, 51, 103
　boroughs, 52, 62, 72, 79, 84, 88,
　　106, 130, 139-46
Long, J., 98, 112, 113
Lupton, T., 7, 8
Lynch, B., 106

McKinsey and Co. Inc., 22-3, 29
McNeil, K., 117
management board, 19
　services, 85
　team, 2, 6, 13, 21-2, 28, 38, 45,
　　50, 51, 53-4, 56-7,
　　61-2, 67, 72-3, 78, 80-5,
　　86-7, 89, 92-4, 107, 122,
　　170
　collective responsibility of, 73,
　　79, 83
Manchester, 96, 170
Mason, T., 4, 43, 45
Maud Committee, *see* Committee
　on Management in Local
　Government
metropolitan counties, 52, 62, 72,
　79, 84, 88, 130, 133-4,
　159-60, 161-5 *passim*
metropolitan districts, 38, 41-2,
　52, 62, 72, 79, 84, 88, 96, 102,
　114, 116, 127-8, 130, 133-4,
　139-46, 159-65 *passim*
Meyer, M.W., 109
mining communities, 102
Moser, C.A., 128
museums, 18

Newark, 96
Newcastle, 16
Newton, K., 109, 121
North Devon, 55
Northumberland, 150
Norton, A., 18, 19
Nottingham, 151

organization structure,
    concentrated, 3, 22, 25-7,
    57-65, 68-90 *passim,* 95,
    106-7, 112-13, 121, 131-55
    passim; see also style of
    integration
    configuration of, 2
    deconcentrated, 3, 22, 29,
    68-90 *passim,* 104, 111,
    113, 131-55 *passim; see
    also* style of integration
    fragmentation, 4, 13, 107
    multi-functional, 9; *see also*
    technology
    performance, 167-9
    variation of, 3-4, 156-72
organizational characteristics, 100,
    109-23, 129-39, 161-4
Ostergaard, G.N., 120

Page, H., 43
parish council, 42
party caucus, 75, 121-2, 131
Paterson Advisory Group, 5, 28,
    39, 76
performance review, 77, 84
Perlman, M., 106
Perrow, C., 114-15
personnel, 72, 76, 77, 79-80,
    84-5, 104, 111-12
Pettigrew, A., 112
Pfeffer, J., 100
Plaid Cymru, 130
planning, 18, 23, 25, 41, 130, 134
police, 130
policy committee, 2, 12, 20, 22-4,
    26, 29, 48-9, 51, 58-62, 67,
    72-3, 75, 79, 84-6, 90, 94,
    113-14, 117, 122-3, 157, 170
    one-party, 49, 74, 79

policy-making, 14, 15
    coordination of, 16, 19-21, 29,
    38, 48, 54, 64, 86, 90, 103,
    108, 112, 116, 122, 137
political organization, 121-2,
    131-2, 135-55 *passim,*
    161-4, 166-7
political complexion, 121-3, 139,
    161-4; *see also* Conservative
    Party, Labour Party
population structure, 126-8
Powys, 150
professionalism, 39, 71
programme area, 23, 25, 46, 50, 64,
    82, 92
    budgetting, 40
    committee, 28, 39-41
    coordination, 76
public accountability, 109, 110,
    117-23, 129, 130, 135
    protection, 18, 24, 46
    relations, 80, 111
Pugh, D.S., 112, 117

Radnor, 146
Ranson, S., 172
rates, 120
Rate Support Grant, 105-6
recreation (and leisure), 3, 24, 39,
    41-2, 81, 92, 130
Redcliffe-Maud, Lord, 2
rent, 120
Rhodes, R.A.W., 74, 121
Richards, P.G., 2, 4
Richer, P., 112-13
Ridley, F.F., 110
Rosenzweig, J.E., 7-8
routineness, 115
Rowan, P., 56
Royal Commission on Local
    Government in England
    1966-1969, 45
rural district councils, 35

Saunders, P., 108
Schoderbek, P.B., 115
Schoenherr, R., 112
Scotland, 28

Scott, W., 128
Secretary, 58-9, 94
Self, P., 9, 110
Sellars, M., 106, 129
'separatist' local authorities, 15
Sharpe, L.J., 1
shire, county, 41, 52, 62, 79, 84, 88,
   128, 130, 133-9, 159-65
     passim
   district, 38, 41, 52, 62-3, 69, 77,
     78-9, 84, 88, 94, 96, 116,
     127, 129-30, 133-4,
     146-52, 159-65 *passim*
   size of authority, 7, 34, 95-6, 101,
     109-14, 116, 125-6, 129,
     132, 137-55 *passim,* 161-4
     passim, 166-7
Skinner, D., 95
Skitt, J., 21
Sloan, A.P., Jr., 107, 166
Smith, A.D., 21
Smith, R., 95
Smith, T. Dan, 2
social services, 24, 26, 41-2, 81,
   111, 130, 135
socio-demographic approach, 100
solace, 163
Solihull, 166
Southampton, 163
specialization, 34, 38, 71, 101,
   113-14
Stalker, G.M., 100, 115, 168, 169
Steers, R.M., 168
Stewart, J.D., 5, 6, 15, 18-19, 21,
   40, 43, 45, 108, 122, 163
Stinchcombe, A.L., 168
Stockport, 42, 94
strategic choice, 8, 157 ff.
Strauss, G., 112
Sutcliffe, A., 95, 121
Sutton, 93

technological services, 18, 41
technology (type of authority), 7,
   109, 110, 114-17, 129
   task (functional) diversity, 116,
     126, 129-30, 132-4, 166
   task predictability, 115
Tivey, L.J., 120
Tolmers Square, 108
Tower Hamlets, 166
townhalls (mini), 45, 93
transportation, 24, 42, 46, 130
treasurer, 23, 25, 56, 58, 76, 78
Treasury, 118-19

urban district councils, 35
Urwick Orr and Partners Ltd., 49

value of local government, 1

Walker, C.J., 115
Walton, R.F., 112
Warkov, S., 116
Warwick, D.P., 166
Wates, N., 95, 108
Webber, R., 128
Weber, M., 168
Webster, B., 43
weights and measures, 15, 39
welfare, 18
West Midlands, 46
West Norfolk, 43-4
Whisler, T.L., 115
Woodward, J., 8, 114-15, 117,
   119, 168
works, 18, 24, 42
Wright, M.W., 99

Zald, M.N., 103
Zwerman, W.L., 115